how2become

A Police Special Constable

Visit www.how2become.co.uk
for more Police Special Constable
titles and career guides

Orders: Please contact How2become Ltd, Suite 2, 50 Churchill Square Business Centre, Kings Hill, Kent ME19 4YU. You can order via the e-mail address info@how2become.co.uk or through Gardners Books at Gardners.com

ISBN: 978-1-907558-90-0

Typeset for How2become Ltd by Molly Hill, Canada.

Printed in Great Britain for How2become Ltd by Bell & Bain Ltd, 303 Burnfield Road, Thornliebank, Glasgow G46 7UQ.

how2become

Attend a 1-Day Police Officer course run by former Police Officers at:

www.PoliceCourse.co.uk

CONTENTS

INTRODUCTION

Welcome to How2become a Police Special Constable.

This guide has been designed to help you prepare for, and pass, the Police Special Constable selection process.

The guide itself has been split up into useful sections to make it easier for you to prepare for each stage. Read each section carefully and take notes as you progress. Don't ever give up on your dreams; if you really want to become a Police Special Constable then you can do it. The way to approach the selection process is to embark on a programme of 'in depth' preparation, and this guide will show you exactly how to do that.

The selection process is not easy to pass, simply because there are many people now applying to become a Special Constable. Your preparation must be focused in the right areas, and also be comprehensive enough to give you every chance of success. This guide will teach you how to be a successful candidate.

The way to pass the selection process is to develop your own

skills and experiences around the core competencies that are required to become a Police Special Constable. Many candidates who apply to join the police will be unaware that the core competencies even exist. As you progress through this guide you will find that these important elements of the role will form the foundations of your preparation. So, the first step in your preparation, and before we go any further, is to get hold of a copy of the core competencies for becoming a Police Special. They will usually form part of your application pack but if they don't, you can obtain a copy of them by visiting the website of the force you are applying to join.

If you need any further help with any elements of the selection process, including application form, written test and interview, then we offer a wide range of products to assist you. These are all available through our online shop www.how2become.co.uk.

Once again, thank you for your custom and we wish you every success in your pursuit to becoming a Police Special Constable.

Work hard, stay focused and be what you want…

Best wishes,

The how2become team

The How2become Team

CHAPTER ONE

THE POLICE SPECIAL CONSTABLE SELECTION PROCESS

During this section of the guide we will cover the selection process for becoming a Police Special Constable.

It is important to note that, whilst many police forces will follow the national selection process, some will use variations of this. As such, we strongly recommend that you confirm the selection process that you will have to take before commencing your preparation. However, the following information will be a good basis for you to start.

PRE-APPLICATION/ELIGIBILITY REQUIREMENTS

In order to become a Police Special Constable you must be aged 18-57 and be capable of meeting the physical and mental demands of the role. During the selection process

you will be assessed against your ability to match the core competencies and also your fitness levels.

You can be of any nationality to become a special; however, you must have the permanent right to remain in the UK if you are from a non-EEA country and have been resident in the UK for the three years before you apply. You are required to possess a good standard of English, have a presentable appearance, be compassionate and tactile and be able to commit to at least 200 hours per year. These commitment levels may vary from force to force so be please check with your chosen force before applying to ensure you can meet their requirements.

It is also important to note that there are a number of jobs that are not compatible with being a Special Constable and you should check these first with your chosen force before applying.

STEP 1: COMPLETE THE SPECIAL CONSTABLE APPLICATION FORM

To apply to be a Police Special Constable you will be required to complete an application. Many forces are now starting to use an online system which will require you to use a keyboard and computer in order to complete the form in its entirety. However, you may find that some forces are still using a paper-based version.

STEP 2: PAPER SIFT PROCESS & PNC CHECK

Once you have submitted your application form you will normally go through a paper sift process and a PNC check. During the sift your application will be checked to see that you meet the minimum eligibility requirements and also that

you have provided suitable evidence to suggest that you can meet the core competencies assessed for the role.

Once your application passes the initial sift an initial PNC (Police National Computer) check will be carried out on you and your background.

STEP 3: ASSESSMENT AND SELECTION DAY

Once you have successfully completed step 2, you will be required to complete an assessment and selection day. Some forces, more notably the Metropolitan Police, will do this over a 2-day period, with the two days being separated out over a short period of time.

As previously mentioned, the selection process for becoming a Police Special can vary from force to force. However, here are some details about the types of assessment you may be required to undertake:

- Police Initial Recruitment Test (PIRT)
- Written test
- Interactivity Test
- Interview

If you are successful at assessment then:

- Medical appointment
- Fitness Test

If you are successful at the fitness test stage, you will be offered a position on the next Special Constable's course, subject to satisfactory references and security checks.

Before we move on to the different sections of this guide, and in particular each element of the selection process, it is

important to explain to you how we intend to teach you to pass the Police Special selection process.

To make it easier to explain, we will break down your preparation into the following key areas:

LEARN ABOUT THE ROLE OF A POLICE SPECIAL CONSTABLE

Before you begin to even complete the application form, it is essential that you learn about the role of a Police Special. This is for a number of reasons. The first reason is that you want to be 100% certain that this job is for you. We know a few people who have joined the police only to leave a few months later because 'it wasn't what they expected'.

The second reason is that it will help you to pass the selection process. If you understand what the role of a Police Special really involves, and not what you may think it involves, then you will find the selection process far easier. This is particularly true in the case of the interactive exercises and interview.

There are a number of ways that you can learn about the role of a Police Special Constable but probably the most effective one is through the website of the force you are applying to join. They will normally have a section on their site which provides details of the role you are applying for.

LEARN AND UNDERSTAND THE CORE COMPETENCIES

The Police Special Constable core competencies are the blueprint to the role you will be required to undertake. Just as the foundations for a house to be built on must be firm, the core competencies are the basic skills that a Police Special must be able to master if he/she is to be capable of

performing the role competently.

Throughout this guide we will make reference to the core competencies and we cannot stress enough how important they are. During the selection process you will be assessed against the core competencies at every stage; therefore you must learn them, understand them and most importantly be able to demonstrate them at every stage of selection.

It is important that you obtain a copy of the Police Special Constable core competencies prior to completing the application form. You will also use the core competencies during your preparation for the assessment centre and the interview.

APPLY THE CORE COMPETENCIES TO EVERY STAGE OF SELECTION

You should remember that during the selection process you are learning how to be a successful candidate, not a successful Police Special Constable. Once you pass the selection process, the Police Force will train you to become a competent member of their team. During selection they are looking to see whether or not you have the potential to become a Police Special and they will use the core competencies as a basis for assessment. At every stage of the process you must demonstrate the core competencies and we will show you how to achieve this within this guide.

IMPROVE YOUR FITNESS LEVELS

Surprisingly, most candidates who fail the selection process do so during the fitness tests. They concentrate so much on passing the assessment centre that they neglect the

other important area of fitness. Within this guide you have received a free bonus section entitled 'How to get Police Special Constable fit'. You will find some useful exercises contained within this guide, so make sure you set aside sufficient time to improve your fitness levels. Do not settle for scraping through the fitness tests but instead look to excel. You will find that as your fitness levels increase, so will your confidence and concentration levels. This in turn will help you to pass the selection process.

We strongly believe that if you follow the simple steps above, and you apply the remainder of the information that is contained within this guide, then your chances of passing the selection process will increase tremendously.

CHAPTER TWO

THE TOP 10 INSIDER TIPS AND ADVICE

The following 10 insider tips have been carefully put together to increase your chances of success during the Police Special Constable selection process. Therefore, it is important that you follow them carefully. Whilst some of them will appear obvious they are still important tips which you need to follow.

INSIDER TIP 1 – BE FULLY PREPARED AND FOCUSED

When you are applying for any career it is of vital importance that you prepare yourself fully for every stage of the selection process. What we mean is that you do everything you can to find out what is required of you. For example, most people do not read the guidance notes that accompany the application form, and then they wonder why they fail that particular section.

Make sure you read every bit of information you receive at least twice and understand what is required in order to pass. Things in life do not come easy and you must be prepared to work hard. Go out of your way to prepare – for example, if you are required to undertake an interactive assessment, get a friend or relative to act out a role-play scenario and see how you deal with it.

When completing the application form allocate plenty of time to do it neatly, concisely and correctly. Don't leave it until the night before the closing date (if there is one) to fill out the form as you will be setting out to fail.

Break down your preparation in the following 4 key areas:

Area 1 – Learn about the role of a Police Special Constable.

Area 2 – Learn and understand the core competencies.

Area 3 – Prepare to apply the core competencies to every stage of the selection process.

Area 4 – Improve your physical fitness.

In addition to your preparation strategy, it is also very important to believe in your own abilities and take advantage of the potential that's within you. If you work hard then you will be rewarded!

Whenever you come up against hurdles or difficult situations and experiences, always try to look for the opportunity to improve yourself. For example, if you have applied for the police previously and failed, what have you done to improve your chances of success the second time around? Did you find out what areas you failed on and have you done anything to improve?

INSIDER TIP 2 – UNDERSTAND AND BELIEVE IN EQUALITY AND FAIRNESS, AND BE ABLE TO DEMONSTRATE IT DURING THE SELECTION PROCESS

Equality and fairness are crucial in today's society. We must treat each other with respect, dignity and understand that people come from different backgrounds and cultures to our own.

Treat people how you expect to be treated – with dignity and respect. If you do not believe in equality, fairness and dignity, then you are applying for the wrong job. Police Special Constables are role models within society and people will look to you to set an example. For example, you wouldn't expect to see a Police Special bullying or shouting at a member of the public in an aggressive manner, would you? As a Police Special Constable you will only use force in exceptional circumstances. You will be required to use your interpersonal skills to diffuse situations and you will need to treat people fairly and equally at all times.

During the selection process your understanding and knowledge of equality and fairness issues will be tested on the application form, at the written tests and also during the interview and role-play scenarios (if applicable). The core competency that relates to respect for race and diversity is the most important and you will not only have to learn it, but also believe in it.

INSIDER TIP 3 – BE PHYSICALLY AND MENTALLY FIT

Being prepared, both physically and mentally, is important if you are to succeed in your application to become a Police Special Constable. Even if you only have a few weeks to prepare, there are lots of ways in which you can improve your

how2become

chances of success.

Many people who successfully pass the selection process are physically fit. Being physically fit has plenty of advantages in addition to simply improving your health. For example, raised self-esteem and confidence in your appearance are also benefits to keeping fit. A person with good health and fitness generally shines when it comes to how they look, how they treat others, and how they go about their day-to-day activities.

In addition to the above, the benefits of 'fitness of mind' are equally as important when tackling the selection process. When applying to join the police you will be learning new skills and developing old ones. The fitter your mind, the easier this will be. If you are fit, both physically and mentally, then you will be able to prepare for longer. You will find that your stamina levels will increase and therefore your ability to practise and prepare will increase too.

Your free *'How to get Police Special Constable fit'* guide provides you with a number of different exercises to choose from in order to prepare yourself for the fitness tests. A little bit each day will go a long way to helping you achieve your goal.

If you prepare yourself fully for the selection process then you will feel more confident on the day, especially when you are under pressure. Make sure you also get plenty of sleep in the build up to selection and ensure you eat a healthy balanced diet.

Many of us underestimate the importance of a healthy diet. The saying *'we are what we eat'* makes a lot of sense and you will find that if you just spend a week or two eating and drinking the right things you will begin to look and feel

healthier. Avoid junk food, alcohol and cigarettes during your preparation and your concentration levels will increase greatly, helping you to get the most out of the work you put in.

Give yourself every opportunity to succeed!

INSIDER TIP 4 – LEARN ABOUT THE POLICE FORCE YOU ARE APPLYING TO JOIN

This is important for a number of reasons. To begin with, you may be asked a question on the application form that relates to your knowledge of the role of a Police Special Constable and also why you want to join that particular force. The Police Force you are applying to join wants to know what exactly attracts you to them. In order to be able to provide a good response to this type of question, you will need to carry out some research.

Most Police Forces have a website. Visit their website and find out what they are doing in terms of community policing. Remember that the job of a Police Special Constable is not just about catching criminals. It is about delivering the best possible service to the public and responding to their needs. Understanding what the police in your area are trying to achieve will demonstrate enthusiasm, commitment and an understanding of what your job will involve, if you are successful.

If you were interviewing a candidate for employment in your Police Force, what would you expect to them to know about your organisation? You would probably expect them to know great deal of information. Learn as much information as possible about the force you are applying to join and be extremely thorough in your preparation.

INSIDER TIP 5 – LEARN AND UNDERSTAND THE CORE COMPETENCIES

VERY IMPORTANT – DO NOT IGNORE

The Police Special Constable core competencies form the fundamental requirements of the role. They identify how you should perform and they are key to the role of a Police Special. Read them carefully and make sure you understand them, they are crucial to your success!

Throughout the selection process you should concentrate on the core competencies, constantly trying to demonstrate them at every stage.

When completing the application form your answers should be based around the core competencies. The same rule applies to the written tests, the interview and also the role-play exercises (if applicable). The most effective way to achieve this is to use 'keywords and phrases' in your responses to the application form and interview questions. You can also adopt this method when tackling the role-plays and the written tests. Using keywords and phrases that correspond to the core competencies will gain you higher scores. Within this guide we will show you how to achieve this, but the first step is for you to learn the core competencies yourself.

Make sure you have a copy of the competencies next to you when completing the application form and whilst preparing for the assessment centre.

The core competencies cover a wide range of required skills and attributes including team working, customer focus, problem solving and equality and fairness issues, to name but a few.

This is the most important tip we can provide you with – Do not ignore it!

 how2become

INSIDER TIP 6 – BE PATIENT AND LEARN FROM YOUR MISTAKES

We can all become impatient when we really want something in life but sometimes it may take us a little longer than expected to reach our goals.

Try to understand that the Police Force receives many thousands of applications each year and it takes time for them to process each one. Only contact the Police Force to chase up your application form if a few weeks have passed and you have not yet heard anything. Most forces will have a recruitment line which you can contact them through.

Whilst waiting to hear if your application form has been successful, use the time wisely and concentrate on the next stage of the selection process. For example, as soon as you submit your application form, start working on your preparation for the assessment centre. 99% of candidates will not start their preparation for the assessment centre until they receive their application results. They can't be bothered to prepare for the next stage until they receive conformation that they've been successful, and as a result, they are missing out on a few extra weeks practise time.

INSIDER TIP 7 – UNDERSTAND DIVERSITY AND THE BENEFITS IT BRINGS TO A WORKFORCE AND SOCIETY

A diverse community has great benefits and the same can be said for a diverse workforce.

The Police Force is no exception and it needs to represent the community in which it serves. If society itself is multi-cultural, then the Police Force needs to be too, if it is to provide the best possible service to the community in which it serves.

Ask yourself the question "What is diversity?" If you cannot answer it then you need to find out as you should be aware of its meaning whilst working in the role of Police Special Constable.

The Police Force must uphold the law fairly and appropriately to protect, respect, help and reassure everyone in all communities. The Police Force must also meet all of the current legislative requirements concerning human rights, race, disability and all employment law that relates to equality.

The focus of the Police Force is to provide a service that responds to the needs of all communities, ensuring the promotion of fair working practices at all times. The concept of diversity encompasses acceptance and respect. It means understanding that each individual is unique, and recognising our individual differences. These can be along the dimensions of race, ethnicity, gender, sexual orientation, socio-economic status, age, physical abilities, religious beliefs, political beliefs, or other ideologies. It is about understanding each other and moving beyond simple tolerance to embracing and celebrating the rich dimensions of diversity contained within each individual.

Learn, understand and believe in diversity. It is important during the selection process and even more important in relation to your role as a Police Special Constable.

INSIDER TIP 8 – DO NOT GIVE UP UNTIL YOU HAVE REACHED YOUR GOAL

If you don't reach the required standard at the first or subsequent attempts, don't give up. So long as you always try to better yourself, there is always the chance that you will succeed. If you do fail any of the stages look at the area(s) you need to improve on.

Did you fail the fitness test? If so, then there are ways of improving. Don't just sit back and wait for the next opportunity to come along, prepare for it straight away and you'll increase your chances for next time.

Many people give up on their goals far too easily. Learning to find the positive aspects of negative situations is a difficult thing to do but a skill that anyone can acquire through practice and determination.

If you really want to achieve your goals
then anything is possible.

During your preparation set yourself small targets each week. For example, your first week may be used to concentrate on learning the core competencies. Your second week can be used to prepare for your written responses on the application form and so on.

If you get tired or feel de-motivated at any time during your preparation, walk away from it and give yourself a break. You may find that you come back to it re-energised, more focused and determined to succeed!

INSIDER TIP 9 – PRACTICE THE ROLE-PLAY EXERCISES WITH A FRIEND OR RELATIVE

Not all Police Forces will require you to undertake a role play/ interactivity exercise. However, for those people who are required to take this element of assessment, read on.

The role-play scenarios can be a daunting experience, especially if you've never done anything like this before. Whilst the Police Force will advise you to be yourself, there are ways in which you can prepare and subsequently increase your chances of success.

The way to prepare for the role-plays is to act them out in a room with a friend or relative. Within this guide you have been provided with a small number of example role-play scenarios. Use these to practise with, and hone your skills in each area of the core competencies that are being assessed.

The only way that you will be able to understand what is required during the role-play exercises is to learn the assessable core competencies. For example, if you are being assessed against the core competency of customer focus, then you will need to demonstrate the following during each role-play scenario:

- Be professional and present an appropriate image in line with your brief and job description.

- Focus on the needs of the customer in every scenario.

- Sort out any problems as soon as possible and apologise for any errors or mistakes that have been made.

- Ask the customer whether they are satisfied with your actions or not. If they are not, then take alternative steps to make them satisfied if possible.

- Keep the customer updated on progress.

Doing all of the above, in addition to covering the other assessable areas, can be quite a difficult task. However, if you practise these skills regularly in the build up to your assessment then you will find it becomes easier and easier the more that you do.

INSIDER TIP 10 – PRACTISE A MOCK INTERVIEW

Mock interviews are a fantastic way to prepare for the assessment centre interview. We recommend that you carry out a mock interview with a friend or relative and try to answer the questions that are contained within this guide.

We also strongly recommend that you sit down in front of a long mirror and respond to the same set of interview questions. Watch your interview technique. Do you slouch? Do you fidget and do you overuse your hands?

It is important that you work on your interview technique during the build up to the assessment centre interview.

Do not make the mistake of carrying out little or no preparation, because you can be guaranteed that some of the other candidates will have prepared fully. Make sure you put in the time and effort and practise a number of mock interviews. You will be amazed at how confident you feel during the real interview.

FREE BONUS TIP – THE USE OF SOCIAL MEDIA

Social network sites such as Facebook and MySpace can hinder and even stop your application. After you have made it through the recruitment assessment centre you will undertake various vetting checks. These involve checks into your background such as your criminal record and your financial status. These are normally just a formality for most candidates.

However, as part of the vetting process your **FACEBOOK**, **MY SPACE**, **TWITTER** and other social networks sites may be checked, and this includes the headlines that you put on your status and pictures that you have uploaded to your

profile. This of course is only possible if your social media account is unlocked and accessible to third parties. We have been reliably informed that some applications have been rejected because of certain pictures and headlines that applicants had on their Facebook account.

While many candidates would not even think that this would be checked, you now have the insider knowledge and can ensure there is nothing on your profile that may prohibit your progression.

The last thing you want to do is get all the way through the assessment centre and then fail in the vetting stage because you have pictures or headlines that are inappropriate. Ensure that your Facebook account is locked to prevent it from being searched by third parties.

CHAPTER THREE

HOW TO COMPLETE THE APPLICATION FORM

INTRODUCTION

The application form is the first stage of the selection process for becoming a Police Special Constable. During this section we will provide you with a step-by-step approach to completing a successful application. It is important to point out that we have used a number of the more common types of application form questions within this section and it is your responsibility to confirm that they relate to your particular form. We have deliberately not made reference to any sections of the form that relate to personal details, simply because what you write here is based on you and you alone.

You will be asked a number of questions on the application form and on the following pages we have provided you with

some tips and advice on how to approach these questions. Please remember that these are provided as a guide only and you should base your answers around your own experiences in both work life and personal life. Questions that are based around 'knowledge, skills and experience' are looking for you to demonstrate that you can meet the requirements of the 'core competencies' for the job you are applying for. Therefore, your answer should match these as closely as possible.

Essentially, the role of a Police Special Constable is made up of a number of core competencies. You may receive these in your application pack or alternatively they can usually be found on the website of the force you are applying to join. Whatever you do, make sure you get a copy of them, and have them by your side when completing the application form. Basically you are looking to match your responses with the assessable core competencies.

Once you have found the 'core competencies', now is the time to structure your answer around these, ensuring that you briefly cover each area based upon your own experiences in both your work life and personal life.

The core competencies that form the basis of the Police Special Constable role are similar to the following. Please note that the core competencies can and do change from time to time, so it is important to confirm that they are correct.

RESPECT FOR RACE AND DIVERSITY

This essentially involves considering and showing respect for the opinions, circumstances and feelings of colleagues and members of the public, no matter what their race, religion, position, background, circumstances, status or appearance.

We have already touched on this important subject and you will no doubt be aware of how important it is to the role of a Police Special.

TEAM WORKING AND WORKING WITH OTHERS

Police Special Constables must be able to work in teams as well as having an ability to work on their own, unsupervised. In order to meet this core competency you will need to be able to develop strong working relationships both inside and outside the team. If there are barriers between different groups then you will need to have the skills to break them down and involve other people in discussions and decisions that you make.

COMMUNITY AND CUSTOMER FOCUS

As a Police Special Constable you must focus on the customer. The customer is essentially the members of the public whom you will be dealing with. You will need to be capable of providing a high-quality service that is tailored to meet each person's individual needs. Throughout the selection process you will be assessed on this area and we have already looked at this core competency in relation to the role-play exercises during insider tip number 9.

The only way that you can provide a high quality service to the public is by understanding the needs of your community. Once you understand the needs of your community then you will be able to provide an excellent service.

EFFECTIVE COMMUNICATION

Police Special Constables must be able to communicate both verbally and in writing. You will also need to communicate to the people you are addressing in a style and manner that is appropriate. This can sometimes be difficult but with practice, it can be achieved.

As a serving Special Constable you will be required to take accurate notes of incidents that you attend. Therefore, the Police Force that you are applying to join will want to assess your potential in this area during the written tests element of the selection process.

PROBLEM SOLVING

In order to solve problems effectively you will first need to gather sufficient information. This can usually be achieved through a number of sources. For example, if you were investigating a burglary, you would first want to gather witness statements from the owner of the property and also the owners of surrounding properties. This information may then lead to other information sources, which will allow you to gather sufficient evidence to make decisions that will ultimately lead to the problem being solved through effective decision-making.

PERSONAL RESPONSIBILITY

Police Special Constables have a reputation for getting things done. They are very good at taking personal responsibility for making things happen and achieving results. In order to effectively achieve this you will need to display a level of motivation, commitment, perseverance and

conscientiousness. At all times you will need to act with a high degree of integrity.

RESILIENCE

As a Police Special you will no doubt be faced with difficult and pressurised circumstances. It is during these tough situations that you will need to show resilience. For example, imagine turning up to a 999 call where a group of drunken lads are refusing to leave a pub after closing time. How would you deal with the situation? You must be prepared to make difficult decisions and have the confidence to see them through.

Now that we have taken a brief look at the core competencies, we can start to look at some of the application form questions. But before we do this, take a read of the following important tips, which will help you to submit a first class application.

- Make sure you read the whole of the application form at least twice before preparing your responses, including the guidance notes.

- Read and understand the person specification and the Police Special Constable core competencies.

- Try to tailor your answers around the 'core competencies' and include any keywords or phrases you think are relevant.

- Make sure you base your answers on actual events that you have experienced either in your work life or personal life.

- Fill the form out in the correct ink colour if you are required to complete a paper-based form. If you fail to

follow this simple instruction then your form may end up in the bin.

- If there is a specific word count for each question, make sure you stick to it.

- Make sure you keep a photocopy of your completed application form before sending it off as you could be asked questions relating to it during the interview stage if you progress that far.

- Be honest when completing the form.

- Get someone to read your completed application form to check for spelling/grammar mistakes. You will lose marks for poor grammar/spelling.

- Finally, send your application form recorded delivery if you are completing a form offline. This will prevent your form going missing in the post, which happens more often that you think.

SAMPLE APPLICATION FORM QUESTIONS AND RESPONSES

The following sample application form questions may not be applicable to your specific form. However, they will provide you with some excellent tips and advice on how to approach the questions. We have supplied you sample questions and answers to a number of the more common types of question.

SAMPLE QUESTION NUMBER 1

What knowledge, skills and experiences do you have that will enable you to meet the requirements of a Police Special Constable?

ANSWER (example only)

"In my previous employment as a customer services assistant I was required to work closely with the general public on many occasions. Often I would be required to provide varied solutions to customers' problems or complaints after listening to their concerns. It was always important for me to listen carefully to what they had to say and respond in a manner that was both respectful and understanding.

On some occasions I would have to communicate with members of the public from a different race or background and I made sure I paid particular attention to making sure they understood how I was going to resolve their problems for them. I would always be sensitive to how they may have been feeling on the other end of the telephone.

Every Monday morning the team that I was a part of would hold a meeting to discuss ways in which we could improve our service to the customer. During these meetings I would always ensure that I contributed and shared any relevant experiences I had had during the previous week. Sometimes

during the group discussions I would find that some members of the group were shy and not very confident at coming forward, so I always sensitively tried to involve them wherever possible.

I remember on one occasion during a meeting I provided a solution to a problem that had been on-going for some time. I had noticed that customers would often call back to see if their complaint had been resolved, which was often time-consuming for the company to deal with. So I suggested that we should have a system where customers were called back after 48 hours with an update of progress in relation to their complaint. My suggestion was taken forward and is now an integral part of the company's procedures. I found it quite hard at first to persuade managers to take on my idea but I was confident that the change would provide a better service to the public we were serving."

First of all read the example answer we have provided above. Then try to 'match' the answer to the core competencies that are relevant to the role of a Police Special Constable and you will begin to understand what is required.

For example, the first paragraph reads as follows:

"In my previous employment as a customer services assistant I was required to work closely with the general public on many occasions. Often I would be required to provide varied solutions to customers' problems or complaints after listening to their concerns. It was always important for me to listen carefully to what they had to say and respond in a manner that was both respectful and understanding."

The above paragraph matches elements of the core competency of community and customer focus.

Now take a look at the next paragraph:

"On some occasions I would have to communicate with members of the public from a different race or background and I made sure I paid particular attention to making sure they understood how I was going to resolve their problems for them. I would always be sensitive to how they may have been feeling on the other end of the telephone."

The response matches elements of the core competency of respect for race and diversity.

Hopefully you are now beginning to understand what is required and how important it is to 'match' your response with the core competencies that are being assessed. Remember to make sure you read fully the guidance notes that are contained within your application pack.

It is also possible to use examples from your personal life, so don't just think about work experiences but look at other aspects of your life too. Try also to think of any community work that you have been involved in. Maybe you are a member of neighbourhood watch and if so you should find it quite a simple process to match the core competencies.

Try to tailor your responses to the core competencies that are being assessed and briefly cover each assessable area if possible. You may also want to try to include keywords and phrases from the core competencies when constructing your response.

We have now provided a number of sample keywords and phrases that are relevant to each core competency. These will help you to understand exactly what we mean when we say 'match' the core competencies in each of your responses.

KEYWORDS AND PHRASES TO CONSIDER USING IN YOUR RESPONSES TO THE APPLICATION FORM QUESTIONS

Respect for race and diversity

- Show respect for others
- Take into account the feelings of colleagues

Team working

- Develop strong working relationships
- Achieve common goals
- Break down barriers
- Involve others

Community and customer focus

- Focusing on the customer
- High-quality service
- The needs of others
- Understand the community
- Commitment

Effective communication

- Communicates ideas
- Effective communication
- Understand others

Problem solving

- Gather information
- Analyse information
- Identify problems
- Make effective decisions

Personal responsibility
- Take personal responsibility
- Achieve results
- Motivation
- Commitment
- Perseverance
- Conscientiousness
- Act with a high degree of integrity

Resilience
- Make difficult decisions
- Confidence

Now let's move on to some more sample application form interview questions and responses.

SAMPLE QUESTION NUMBER 2

Why have you applied for this post and what do you have to offer?

Some Police Force application forms may ask you questions based around the question above. If so, then you need to answer again in conjunction with the 'person spec' relevant to that particular force.

An example answer for the above question could be based around the following:

"I believe my personal qualities and attributes would be suited to that of a Police Special Constable within this Constabulary. I enjoy working in a diverse organisation that offers many and varied challenges. I would enjoy the challenge of working in

a customer-focused environment that requires a high level of personal responsibility, openness to change and teamwork. I have a high level of commitment, motivation and integrity, which I believe would help the Police Force respond to the needs of their community."

Top tips

- The length of response that you provide should be dictated by the amount of space available to you on the application form or the specified number of maximum words.

- The form itself may provide you with the facility to attach a separate sheet if necessary. If it doesn't then make sure you keep to the space provided.

- The best tip we can give you is to write down your answer first in rough before committing your answer to paper on the actual application form. This will allow you to iron out any mistakes.

SAMPLE QUESTION NUMBER 3

It is essential that Police Special Constables are capable of showing respect for other people regardless of their background. Please describe a situation when you have challenged someone's behaviour that was bullying, discriminatory or insensitive. You will be assessed on how positively you acted during the situation, and also on how well you understood what had occurred.

PART 1 – Describe the situation and also tell us about the other person or people who were involved.

"Whilst working as a sales person for my previous employer, I was serving a lady who was from an ethnic background. I

was helping her to choose a gift for her son's 7th birthday when a group of four youths entered the shop and began looking around at the goods we had for sale.

For some strange reason they began to make racist jokes and comments to the lady. I was naturally offended by the comments and was concerned for the lady to whom these comments were directed.

Any form of bullying and harassment is not welcome in any situation and I was determined to stop it immediately and protect the lady from any more harm."

Top tip

- Try to answer this type of question focusing on the positive action that you took, identifying that you understood the situation. Don't forget to include keywords and phrases in your response that are relevant to the competencies that are being assessed.

- Make sure you are honest in your responses. The situations you provide MUST be real and ones that you took part in.

PART 2 – What did you say and what did you do?

"The lady was clearly upset by their actions and I too found them both offensive and insensitive. I decided to take immediate action and stood between the lady and the youths to try to protect her from any more verbal abuse or comments. I told them in a calm manner that their comments were not welcome and would not be tolerated. I then called over my manager for assistance and asked him to call the police before asking the four youths to leave the shop.

I wanted to diffuse the situation as soon as possible, being constantly aware of the lady's feelings. I was confident that

the shop's CCTV cameras would have picked up the four offending youths and that the police would be able to deal with the situation.

After the youths had left the shop I sat the lady down and made her a cup of tea whilst we waited for the police to arrive. I did everything that I could to support and comfort the lady and told her that I would be prepared to act as a witness to the bullying and harassment that I had just witnessed."

Top tip

- Remember to read the core competencies before constructing your response. What are the police looking for in relation to what you say to others and how you act?

PART 3 – Why do you think the other people behaved as they did?

"I believe it is predominantly down to a lack of understanding, education and awareness. Unless people are educated and understand why these comments are not acceptable then they are not open to change.

They behave in this manner because they are unaware of how dangerous their comments and actions are. They believe it is socially acceptable to act this way when it certainly isn't."

Top tip

- When describing your thoughts or opinions on how others acted in a given situation, keep your personal views separate. Try to provide a response that shows a mature understanding of the situation.

PART 4 – What would have been the consequences if you had not acted as you did?

"The consequences are numerous. To begin with I would have been condoning this type of behaviour and missing an opportunity to let the offenders know that their actions are wrong (educating them). I would have also been letting the lady down, which would have in turn made her feel frightened, hurt and not supported.

We all have the opportunity to help stop discriminatory behaviour and providing we ourselves are not in any physical danger then we should take positive action to stop it."

Top tip

- Try to demonstrate an understanding of what would have possibly happened if you had failed to take action.

SAMPLE QUESTION NUMBER 4

Police Special Constables are required to work in teams and therefore they must be able to work well with others. Please describe a situation when it was necessary to work with other people in order to get something done and achieve a positive result. During this question you will be assessed on how you co-operated with the other members of the team in completing the task in hand.

PART 1 – Tell us what had to be done.

"Whilst driving along the motorway I noticed that an accident had just occurred up in front of me. Two cars were involved in the accident and some people in the car appeared to be injured. There were a number of people stood around looking at the crash and I was concerned that help had not been called.

We needed to work as a team to call the emergency services, look after the injured people in the cars and try to stay as safe as possible."

Top tip

- Make sure you provide a response to the questions that is specific in nature. Do not fall into the trap of telling them what you 'would do' if the situation was to occur.

PART 2 – How was it that you became involved?

"I became involved through pure instinct. I'm not the type of person to sit in the background and let others resolve situations. I prefer to try to help out where I can and I believed that, in this situation, something needed to be done. It was apparent that people were hurt and the emergency services had not been called yet.

There were plenty of people around but they weren't working as a team to get the essentials done."

Top tip

- It is better to say that you volunteered to get involved rather than that you were asked.

PART 3 – What did you do and what did others do?

"I immediately shouted out loud and asked if anybody was a trained first aid person, nurse or doctor. A man came running over and told me that he worked for the British Red Cross and that he had a first aid kit in his car. He told me that he would look after the injured people but that he would need an assistant. I asked a lady if she would help him and she said that she would. I then decided that I needed to call the emergency services and went to use my mobile phone.

At this point a man pointed out to me that if I used the orange emergency phone it would get through quicker and the operator would be able to locate exactly where the accident was. I asked him if he would call the emergency services on the orange phone, as he appeared to know exactly what he was doing. I noticed a lady sat on the embankment next to the hard shoulder crying and she appeared to be a bit shocked.

I asked an onlooker if he would mind sitting with her and talking to her until the ambulance got there. I thought this was important so that she felt supported and not alone.

Once that was done, the remaining onlookers and I decided to work as a team to remove the debris lying in the road, which would hinder the route for the oncoming emergency service vehicles."

Top tip

- Provide a response that is both concise and flows in a logical sequence.

PART 4 – How was it decided how things were going to be done?

"I decided to take the initiative and get everyone working as a team. I asked the people to let me know what their particular strengths were. One person was first aid trained and so he had the task of attending to the injured. Everyone agreed that we needed to work together as a team in order to achieve the task."

PART 5 – What did you do to ensure the team were able to get the result they wanted?

"I took control of a deteriorating situation and got everybody who was stood around doing nothing involved. I made sure I asked if anybody was skilled in certain areas such as first aid

and used the people who had experience, such as the man who knew about the orange emergency telephones.

I also kept talking to everybody and asking them if they were OK and happy with what they were doing. I tried my best to co-ordinate the people with jobs that I felt needed to be done as a priority."

Top tip

- Try to include details that demonstrate how your actions had a positive impact on the result.

PART 6 – What benefit did you see for yourself in what you did?

"The benefit overall was for the injured people, ensuring that they received treatment as soon as possible. However, I did feel a sense of achievement that the team had worked well together even though we had never met each other before. I also learnt a tremendous amount from the experience.

At the end we all shook hands and talked briefly and there was a common sense of achievement amongst everybody that we had done something positive. Without each other we wouldn't have been able to get the job done."

Top tip

- Try to explain that the benefit was positive.

SAMPLE QUESTION NUMBER 5

During very difficult circumstances, Police Special Constables must be able to remain calm and act logically and decisively. Please describe a situation when you have been in a very challenging or difficult situation and had to make a decision where other people disagreed with you.

You will be assessed in this question on how positively you reacted in the face of adversity and challenge.

PART 1 – Tell us about the situation and why you felt it was difficult.

"Whilst working in my current position as a sales person I was the duty manager for the day as my manager had gone sick. It was the week before Christmas and the shop was very busy.

During the day the fire alarm went off and I started to ask everybody to evacuate the shop, which is our company policy. The alarm has gone off in the past but the normal manager usually lets people stay in the shop whilst he finds out if it's a false alarm.

This was a difficult situation because the shop was very busy, nobody wanted to leave and my shop assistants were disagreeing with me in my decision to evacuate the shop. Some of the customers were becoming irate as they were in the changing rooms at the time."

Top tip

- For questions of this nature you will need to focus on the core competency that relates to resilience. Remember to use keywords and phrases in your responses that match the core competencies being assessed.

PART 2 – Who disagreed with you and what did they say or do?

"Both the customers and my shop assistants were disagreeing with me. The customers were saying that it was appalling that they had to evacuate the shop and that they would complain to the head office about it.

The sales staff were trying to persuade me to keep everybody inside the shop and saying that it was most probably a false

alarm as usual. I was determined to evacuate everybody from the shop for safety reasons and would not allow anybody to deter me from my aim.

The safety of my staff and customers was at the forefront of my mind even though it wasn't at theirs."

Top tip

- Do not become aggressive or confrontational when dealing with people who disagree with you. Remain calm at all times but be resilient in your actions if it is right to do so.

PART 3 – What did you say or do?

"Whilst remaining calm and in control I shouted at the top of my voice that everybody was to leave, even though the sound of the alarm was reducing the impact of my voice. I then had to instruct my staff to walk around the shop and tell everybody to leave whilst we investigated the problem.

I had to inform one member of staff that disciplinary action would be taken against him if he did not co-operate. Eventually, after I kept persisting, everybody began to leave the shop. I then went outside with my members of staff, took a roll call and awaited the Fire Brigade to arrive."

Top tip

- Remember to be in control at all times and remain calm. These are qualities that good Police Special Constable will possess.

PART 4 – Tell us how this situation made you feel initially.

"At first I felt a little apprehensive and under pressure but determined not to move from my position as I knew 100% that it was the right one. I was disappointed that my staff

did not initially help me but the more I persisted the more confident I became.

This was the first time I had been the manager of the shop so I felt that this situation tested my courage and determination. By remaining calm I was able to deal with the situation far more effectively."

Top tip

- Do not say that you felt angry and do not use words that are confrontational.

- By staying calm you will be able to deal with situations far more effectively.

PART 5 – How did you feel immediately after the incident?

"I felt good because I had achieved my aim and I had stood by my decision. It made me feel confident that I could do it again and deal with any difficult situation. I now felt that I had the courage to manage the shop better and had proven to myself that I was capable of dealing with difficult situations.

I had learnt that staying calm under pressure improves your chances of a successful outcome dramatically."

SAMPLE QUESTION NUMBER 6

Police Special Constables must deliver an excellent service to the public. It is also important that they build good working relationships with the public and other stakeholders. Describe a situation when you had to deal with someone who was disappointed with the level of service they received. Try to use an occasion where you had contact with that person over a period of time or on a number of different occasions in order to rectify the problem.

PART 1 – Describe the situation and why you think the person was not happy.

"Whilst working as a sales person in my current job, I was approached by an unhappy customer. He explained to me, in an angry manner, that he had bought a pair of running trainers for his daughter's birthday the week before. When she unwrapped her present the morning of her birthday she noticed that one of the training shoes was a size 6 whilst the other one was a size 7.

Understandably he was not happy with the level of service that he had received from our company. The reason for his dissatisfaction was that his daughter had been let down on her birthday and as a consequence he then had to travel back into town to sort out a problem that should not have occurred in the first place."

Top tip

- In order to respond to this type of question accurately you will need to study and understand the core competency that relates to customer focus.

- Make sure you answer the question in two parts. Describe the situation and then explain why the person was not happy.

PART 2 – Explain what you did in response to his concerns.

"Immediately I tried to diffuse his anger by telling him that I fully understood his situation and that I would feel exactly the same if I was in his position. I promised him that I would resolve the situation and offered him a cup of tea or coffee whilst he waited for me to address the problem. This appeared to have the effect of calming him down and the tone in his voice became friendlier.

I then spoke to my manager and explained the situation to him. I suggested that maybe it would be a good idea to replace the running shoes with a new pair (both the same size) and also refund the gentleman in full as a gesture to try to make up for our mistake. The manager agreed to my suggestion and so I returned to the gentleman concerned and explained what we proposed to do for him. He was delighted with the good will offer and appeared to calm down totally.

We then went over to the checkout to refund his payment and replace the running shoes. At this point I took down the gentleman's address and telephone number, which is company policy for any goods returned for refund or exchange. The man then left the shop happy with the service he had received.

The following day I telephoned the gentleman at home to check that everything was OK with the running shoes and he told me that his daughter was delighted. He also informed me that despite the initial bad experience he would still use our shop in the future."

Top tip

- Remember that customer focus is an important element of the role of a Police Special Constable. You must focus on the needs of the customer at all times.

PART 3 – How did you know that the person was happy with what you did?

"I could detect a change in his behaviour as soon as I explained that I sympathised with his situation. Again, when I offered him a cup of tea or coffee I detected a change in his behaviour once more.

The tone in his voice became less agitated and angry so

I took advantage of this situation and tried even harder to turn his bad experience with us into a positive one. When we offered him the refund along with the replacement of the running shoes his attitude changed again but this time he appeared to be satisfied.

Finally, when I telephoned him the following day he was so happy that he said he would come back to us again despite the initial poor level of service."

Top tip

- In your response to this part of the question try to indicate that you followed up your actions by contacting the person to see if they were satisfied with what you did for them.

PART 4 – If you hadn't acted like you did what do you think the outcome would have been?

"To begin with I believe the situation would have become even more heated and possibly untenable. His anger or dissatisfaction could have escalated if my attempts to diffuse the situation had not taken place. I also believe that we would have lost a customer and therefore lost future profits and custom for the company. There would have been a high possibility that the gentleman would have taken his complaint higher, either to our head office, trading standards or the local newspaper.

Customer service is important and we need to do everything we can (within reason) to make the level of service we provide as high as possible. I also believe that our reputation could have been damaged as that particular gentleman could have told friends or colleagues not to use our shop in the future, whereas now, he is maybe more inclined to promote us in a positive light instead."

Top tip

- Demonstrate that you have a clear understanding of what would have happened if you had not acted as you did.

- Study the core competency that is relevant to customer focus before answering this question.

- Use keywords and phrases in your response from the core competency that is being assessed.

SAMPLE QUESTION NUMBER 7

Police Special Constables must be organised and manage their own time effectively. Please describe a situation when you were under pressure to carry out a number of tasks at the same time.

Tell us what you had to do, which things were a priority and why.

"Whilst working for a sales company as a manager I had 4 important tasks to complete on the last working day of every month. These tasks included stocktaking reports, approving and submitting the sales reps' mileage claims, auditing the previous month's accounts and planning the strategy for the following month's activity.

My first priority was always to approve and submit the sales reps' mileage claims. If I did not get this right or failed to get them submitted on time the reps would be out of pocket when they received their payslip. This would in turn affect morale and productivity within the office. The second task to complete would be the stocktaking reports.

This was important to complete on time as if I missed the deadline we would not have sufficient stock for the following

month and therefore there would be nothing to sell and customers would not receive their goods on time. The third task would be the strategy for the following month. This was usually a simple task but still important as it would set out my plan for the following month's activities.

Finally I would audit the accounts. The reason why I would leave this task until the end is that they did not have to be submitted to Head Office until the 14th day of the month and therefore I had extra time to complete this task and ensure that I got it right the first time."

Top tip

- Try to demonstrate that you have excellent organisation skills and that you can cope with the demands and pressures of the job.

SAMPLE QUESTION NUMBER 8

Police Special Constables must be capable of communicating effectively with lots of different people, both verbally and in writing.

Please explain a situation when you had to tell an individual or a group of people something that they may have found difficult or distressing. You will be assessed on how well you delivered the message and also on what you took into account when speaking to them.

PART 1 – Who were the people and what did you have to tell them?

"The people involved were my elderly next door neighbours. They had a cat that they had looked after for years and they were very fond of it. I had to inform them that their cat had just been run over by a car in the road."

PART 2 – Why do you think they may have found the message difficult or distressing?

"I was fully aware of how much they loved their cat and I could understand that the message I was about to tell them would have been deeply distressing. They had cherished the cat for years and to suddenly lose it would have been a great shock to them."

PART 3 – How did you deliver the message?

"To begin with I knocked at their door and ask calmly if I could come in to speak to them. Before I broke the news to them I made them a cup of tea and sat them down in a quiet room away from any distractions. I then carefully and sensitively told them that their cat had passed away following an accident in the road. At all times I took into account their feelings and I made sure I delivered the message sensitively and in a caring manner."

PART 4 – Before you delivered your message, what did you take into account?

"I took into account where and when I was going to deliver the message. It was important to tell them in a quiet room away from any distractions so that they could grieve in peace. I also took into account the tone in which I delivered the message and I also made sure that I was sensitive to their feelings. I also made sure that I would be available to support them after I had broken the news."

Top tip

- Read the question carefully and make sure you answer every element of it.

- Read the core competency that is relevant to effective communication before providing a response to this question.

You may find on the application form that some of the questions are based around different core competencies. If this is the case then simply apply the same process of trying to match the core competencies by using keywords and phrases in your responses.

FINAL TIPS FOR COMPLETING A SUCCESSFUL APPLICATION FORM

Whilst some of the following tips have already been provided within this section, it is important that we provide them again. Your success very much depends on your ability to do the following:

- Read the application form and the guidance notes at least twice before you complete it.

- If possible, photocopy the application form and complete a draft copy first. This will allow you to make any errors or mistakes without being penalised.

- Obtain a copy of the core competencies and have them at your side when completing the form.

- Take your time when completing the form and set aside plenty of time for each question. We recommend that you spend 3-5 evenings completing the application form breaking it down into manageable portions. This will allow you to maintain high levels of concentration.

- If you are required to complete a written version of the form, be sure to complete it in the correct colour ink and follow all instructions very carefully. Your form could be thrown out for simply failing to follow simple instructions.

- Be honest when completing the form and if you are unsure about anything contact the police force for confirmation.

- Try not to make any spelling or grammar errors. You **WILL** lose marks for poor spelling, grammar and punctuation.

- Try to use keywords and phrases in your responses to the assessable questions that are relevant to the core competencies.

- Get someone to check over your form for errors before you submit it. If they can't read your application form, the assessor probably won't be able to either.

- Take a photocopy of your final completed form before submitting it.

- Try to submit the form well before the closing date. Some forces may operate a cut-off point in terms of the number of applications they receive.

- Some forms do get lost in the post so it is advisable that you send it by recorded delivery for peace of mind.

- If your form is unsuccessful ask for feedback, if available. It is important that you learn from your mistakes.

WHAT HAPPENS AFTER I HAVE SENT OFF MY APPLICATION FORM?

Once you have completed and sent off your application form there will be a period before you find out whether or not you have been successful. Some forces will only write to you if you have been successful.

Regardless of the above, it is crucial that you start preparing for the assessment centre even before you receive your result. By starting your preparation early you will effectively be giving yourself a 2-3 week advantage over the other applicants. 99% of applicants will wait to receive their result before they start to prepare. This is where you can gain an advantage.

During the next section you will learn about the assessment centre and the different stages that you may have to go through. Prepare fully for each stage and really go out of your way to improve your skills and knowledge of the selection process.

Please note: the information you are about to read may differ from force to force. Make sure you confirm the exact requirements of your particular assessment centre before you start preparing.

CHAPTER FOUR

HOW TO PASS THE NATIONAL RECRUITMENT ASSESSMENT CENTRE

When preparing to complete the application form you will have already learnt a considerable amount of job specific information that is relevant to the role of a Police Special Constable. Once again, the core competencies are going to form the basis of your preparation and you should have a copy of them next to you when preparing for each stage of the assessment centre.

It is important to point out at this stage that Police Forces up and down the country may vary their assessment centre for Police Specials. However, in order to assist you during your preparation we will cover all of the different elements in this section.

In relation to the written tests preparation, only you will know your current skill level and will therefore need to decide how much time you allocate to this area. The majority of candidates are not overly concerned about the numerical and verbal reasoning tests (if applicable) but they are when it comes to report writing. Within this guide you will receive some invaluable advice relating to every area of assessment so make sure you read it carefully and try out the sample test questions.

The role-play exercises can be a daunting experience. However, if you practise them beforehand, and learn how to demonstrate the core competencies being assessed, then your confidence will increase dramatically. A thorough explanation of how to prepare for them has been provided within this guide. Once again, focus your role-play preparation around the core competencies, as this is how the police will assess you.

Within this guide we have also provided you with information on how to prepare for the Situational Judgement Test and the interview.

We will now break down each assessment centre area in detail to allow you to prepare effectively.

THE WRITTEN TESTS

When preparing for the numerical and verbal reasoning tests (if applicable), the most effective way to increase your scores is to simply practise plenty of sample questions. Within this section we have provided you with a number of sample test questions. In addition to these you may also decide to purchase additional testing resources. If you do decide to pursue this option then we recommend the following:

1. Numerical reasoning and verbal reasoning testing booklets from the website www.how2become.co.uk.

2. Consider practising online tests through the website www.job-test.co.uk.

We have now provided you with a number of practice sample questions that you may encounter during your tests. It is unlikely that you will be asked these exact questions during your assessment, but please do use them as part of your preparation.

Work as quickly as possible through each question and see how well you score. Try to understand each question and read it carefully. The answers to each question are at the end of the exercises.

Use a pen and paper, and answer each question as **TRUE**, **FALSE** or **IMPOSSIBLE TO SAY**.

REMEMBER TO ANSWER YOUR QUESTIONS BASED SOLELY ON THE INFORMATION GIVEN AND NOT ON YOUR OWN OPINIONS OR VIEWS.

VERBAL REASONING QUESTION NUMBER 1

A fire has occurred in a nightclub belonging to Harry James. One person died in the fire, which occurred at 11pm on Saturday night. The club was insured for less than its value.

Questions – TRUE, FALSE or IMPOSSIBLE TO SAY?

1. The fire occurred at 1100 hours.

2. A relative of Harry James was killed in the fire.

3. If the insurance company decide to pay out for the fire, Harry James stands to make a profit.

4. The fire was caused by arson.

5. The club was not insured at the time of the fire

VERBAL REASONING QUESTION NUMBER 2

An accident occurred on the M6 motorway between junctions 8 and 9 southbound at 3pm. The driver of a Ford Fiesta was seen to pull into the middle lane without indicating, forcing another car to veer into the central reservation. One person suffered a broken arm and was taken to hospital before the police arrived.

Questions – TRUE, FALSE or IMPOSSIBLE TO SAY?

1. The accident was on the M6 motorway on the carriageway that leads to Scotland.

2. The driver of the Ford Fiesta was injured in the crash.

3. The central reservation was responsible for the accident.

4. The police did not give first aid at the scene.

5. The accident happened at 1500 hours.

VERBAL REASONING QUESTION NUMBER 3

A man of between 30 and 35 years of age was seen stealing a car from outside Mrs Brown's house yesterday. He was seen breaking the nearside rear window with a hammer before driving off at 40 miles per hour. He narrowly missed a young mother who was pushing a pram.

Questions – TRUE, FALSE or IMPOSSIBLE TO SAY?

1. The man who stole the car was 34 years old.

2. He stole Mrs Brown's car.

3. The young mother who was pushing a pram was injured.

4. He used a hammer to smash the windscreen.

5. When he drove off he was breaking the speed limit.

VERBAL REASONING QUESTION NUMBER 4

A shopkeeper called Mr Smith was seen serving alcohol to a girl aged 16.

The girl had shown him fake ID, which was a driving licence belonging to her sister. The incident occurred at around 11.30pm on a Wednesday evening during December.

Questions – TRUE, FALSE or IMPOSSIBLE TO SAY?

1. The girl is old enough to purchase alcohol from Mr Smith.

2. The girl purchased the alcohol for her sister.

3. The girl's sister had given the driving licence to her.

4. Mr Smith will receive a custodial sentence for his actions.

 how2become

VERBAL REASONING QUESTION NUMBER 5

Following a bank robbery in a town centre, 6 masked gunmen were seen speeding away from the scene in a black van. The incident, which happened in broad daylight in front of hundreds of shoppers, was picked up by CCTV footage. Police are appealing for witnesses. The local newspaper has offered a £5,000 reward for any information leading to the conviction of all the people involved.

Questions – TRUE, FALSE or IMPOSSIBLE TO SAY?

1. The car in which the gunmen drove off was a black van.

2. Someone must have seen something.

3. The incident was picked up by CCTV cameras.

4. The newspaper will pay £5,000 for information leading to the arrest of all of the men involved.

5. Police are not appealing to members of the public for help.

VERBAL REASONING QUESTION NUMBER 6

A factory fire at 'Stevenage Supplies' was arson, the police have confirmed. A man was seen running away from the scene shortly before the fire started. Earlier that day a man was sacked from the company for allegedly stealing money from the safe. The incident is the second one to occur at the factory in as many months.

Questions – TRUE, FALSE or IMPOSSIBLE TO SAY?

1. Police have confirmed that the fire at the factory was arson.

2. The man who was seen running away from the fire was the man who started it.

3. One previous 'fire-related' incident has already occurred at the factory.

4. The man who was sacked from the factory may have started the fire.

VERBAL REASONING QUESTION NUMBER 7

At 1800 hours today police issued a statement in relation to the crime scene in Armstrong Road. Police have been examining the scene all day and reports suggest that it may be murder. Forensic officers have been visiting the incident and inform us that the whole street has been cordoned off and nobody will be allowed through. Police say that the street involved will be closed for another 18 hours and no access will be available to anyone during this time.

Questions – TRUE, FALSE or IMPOSSIBLE TO SAY?

1. Police have confirmed the incident is murder.

2. Forensic officers have now left the scene.

3. The road will be open at 12 noon the following day.

4. Although the street has been cordoned off, taxis and buses will be given access.

5. Forensic officers will be at the scene all night.

VERBAL REASONING QUESTION NUMBER 8

Mrs Rogers telephoned the police at 8pm to report a burglary at her house in Gamble Crescent. She reports that she came home from work and her front bedroom window was open but she doesn't remember leaving it open.

She informs the police that her jewellery box is missing and also £40 cash, which was left on the kitchen table. She came home from work at 5pm and left again at 7am in the morning. No other signs of forced entry were visible.

Questions – TRUE, FALSE or IMPOSSIBLE TO SAY?

1. The burglar made his/her way in through the bedroom window.

2. The burglar took the jewellery and £40 cash before leaving.

3. Mrs Rogers was away from the house for 10 hours in total.

4. Mrs Rogers may have left the window open herself before leaving for work.

5. There were other visible signs of forced entry.

ANSWERS TO VERBAL REASONING QUESTIONS

Question 1

1. False
2. Impossible to say
3. Impossible to say
4. Impossible to say
5. False

Question 2

1. False
2. Impossible to say
3. False
4. True
5. True

Question 3

1. Impossible to say
2. Impossible to say
3. False
4. False
5. Impossible to say

Question 4

1. False
2. Impossible to say
3. Impossible to say
4. Impossible to say

Question 5

1. True
2. Impossible to say
3. True
4. False
5. False

Question 6

1. True
2. Impossible to say
3. True
4. True

Question 7

1. False
2. Impossible to say
3. True
4. False
5. Impossible to say

Question 8

1. Impossible to say
2. Impossible to say
3. False
4. True
5. False

Now that you have had the chance to try out a number of verbal reasoning test questions, hopefully you are beginning to grasp what is required. It is very easy to get caught out when answering these types of questions due to the fact that you have to rely solely on the information provided, something that is integral to role of a Police Special Constable.

Now try the next set of sample verbal reasoning questions.

VERBAL REASONING QUESTION NUMBER 9

The local bank was held up at gunpoint on Monday the 18th of September at approximately 4pm. The thieves used a black motorcycle to make their getaway. The following facts are also known about the incident:

- Two shots were fired.
- There were 12 staff members on duty at the time of the raid.
- The alarm was raised by the manager and the police were called.
- The cashier was ordered to hand over a bag of money containing £7,000.
- The thieves have not yet been caught.
- Police are appealing for witnesses.

Questions – TRUE, FALSE or IMPOSSIBLE TO SAY?

1. The thieves have been caught.
2. The cashier raised the alarm.
3. The cashier was shot.
4. Two people were injured.
5. The bank was open for business at the time of the incident.

VERBAL REASONING QUESTION NUMBER 10

A father and son were found dead in their two-bedroom flat in Sparsbrook on Sunday evening. They had both been suffocated. The following facts are also known:

- The victims were identified by the police as Mark Webster, 16 years old, and his father, Thomas Webster, 39 years old.

- Thomas was in debt to the sum of £37,000.

- Two men were seen leaving the house at 4pm on Sunday afternoon.

- Two men were seen acting suspiciously in the area on Saturday evening before driving off in a Brown Ford Escort car.

- Thomas had previously contacted the police to express his concerns about his safety following threats from his creditors.

- The house had not been broken into.

Questions – TRUE, FALSE or IMPOSSIBLE TO SAY?

1. The people Thomas owed money to could have been responsible for the deaths.

2. The two men seen leaving the house were not responsible for the deaths of Mark Webster and Thomas Webster.

3. The house had been broken into.

4. Neighbours reported two men acting suspiciously in the area on Saturday evening.

5. The people responsible for the deaths drove off in a brown Ford Escort car.

VERBAL REASONING QUESTION NUMBER 11

Firefighters have discovered a large quantity of cannabis during a fire on a farm in the village of Teynsville. Police have cordoned off the area. The following facts are also known about the incident:

- The farm is owned by local farmer Peter Watts.

- The fire was deliberately started.

- Peter Watts has two previous convictions for possession and supply of Class A drugs.

- Peter Watts wife was at home on the night of the fire.

- Peter Watts was visiting friends in the nearby town of Grentshill when the fire started.

- A passer-by reported the fire to the police at 9pm.

- Peter Watts has been arrested on suspicion of possession of cannabis.

Questions – TRUE, FALSE or IMPOSSIBLE TO SAY?

1. Cannabis is a Class A drug.

2. The fire was started accidentally.

3. A passer-by reported the fire to the fire service at 9pm.

4. The cannabis found during the fire belonged to Peter Watts.

5. Peter Watts has been arrested for possession of cannabis.

VERBAL REASONING QUESTION NUMBER 12

A row of terraced houses was partially destroyed by an explosion on the 17th of April 2007. Just before the explosion a man was seen running back into his house. He had reported a gas leak to the gas board 7 days prior to the explosion. The following facts are also known about the incident:

- The smell of gas had also been reported by two further residents in the weeks leading up to the explosion.

- The police are investigating possible terrorist connections with one of the residents.

Questions – TRUE, FALSE or IMPOSSIBLE TO SAY?

1. A gas leak was reported to the gas board on the 10th of April 2007.

2. The explosion was caused by a gas leak.

3. The explosion was not caused by a terrorist attack.

4. The man seen running back into his house had already reported a gas leak to the gas board.

5. The row of terraced houses that were involved in the explosion has been damaged.

ANSWERS TO VERBAL REASONING QUESTIONS

Question number 9
1.   False.
2.   False.
3.   Impossible to say.
4.   Impossible to say.
5.   Impossible to say.

Question number 10
1.   True.
2.   Impossible to say.
3.   False.
4.   Impossible to say.
5.   Impossible to say.

Question number 11
1.   Impossible to say.
2.   False.
3.   False.
4.   Impossible to say.
5.   False.

Question number 12
1.   True.
2.   Impossible to say.
3.   Impossible to say.
4.   True.
5.   True.

TIPS FOR PASSING THE VERBAL REASONING TEST

- In the build up to the assessment, make sure you practise plenty of sample test questions. Little and often is far more effective than cramming the night before your assessment.

- Read the questions carefully. During the test you may have to answer questions that are answered either TRUE, FALSE, or IMPOSSIBLE TO SAY. Base your answers on the evidence supplied only and not on your own views or opinions.

- Do not spend too long on one particular question. If you cannot answer it then move on to the next question but make sure you leave a space on the answer sheet.

- Consider purchasing additional verbal reasoning test booklets or practice aids. You can obtain these through the website www.how2become.co.uk.

- Get plenty of sleep the night before the test. This will allow you to concentrate fully.

NUMERICAL TESTS

As part of the written tests you may also have to sit a numeracy assessment.

The most effective way to prepare for this type of test is to practise sample numerical reasoning tests.

Apart from these sample questions, there are a number of alternative methods for improving your scores. You may wish to invest in a psychometric numerical reasoning test booklet so that you can practise more tests. You can obtain more sample tests through the website www.how2become.co.uk. The more you practise the better you will become at answering these types of questions.

Remember – practice makes perfect!

In the next section we have provided you with a number of sample numeracy tests to help you prepare. Try to answer the questions quickly and without the use of a calculator. You have 5 minutes in which to answer the 14 questions.

NUMERICAL REASONING QUESTIONS – EXERCISE 1

1. A wallet has been found containing one £20 note, five £5 notes, a fifty pence coin and three 2 pence coins. How much is in the wallet?

   Answer [   ]

2. Subtract 200 from 500, add 80, subtract 30 and multiply by 2. What number do you have?

   Answer [   ]

3. A multi-storey car park has 8 floors and can hold 72 cars on each floor. In addition to this there is also allocation for 4 disabled parking spaces per floor. How many spaces are there in the entire car park?

   Answer [   ]

4. A man saves £12.50 per month. How much would he have saved after 1 year?

   Answer [   ]

5. If there have been 60 accidents along one stretch of a motorway in the last year, how many on average have occurred each month?

   Answer [   ]

6. Out of 40,000 applicants only 4,000 are likely to be successful. What percentage will fail?

    Answer [   ]

7. What percentage of 400 is 100?

    Answer [   ]

8. Malcolm's shift commences at 0615 hours. If his shift is 10.5 hours long what time will he finish?

    Answer [   ]

9. If Mary can bake 12 cakes in 2 hours how many will she bake in 10 hours?

    Answer [   ]

10. If there are 24 hours in the day. How many hours are there in one week?

    Answer [   ]

11. Susan has 10 coins and gives 5 of them to Steven and the remainder to Alan. Alan gives 3 of his coins to Steven who in turn gives half of his back to Susan. How many is Susan left with?

    Answer [   ]

12. Add 121 to 54. Now subtract 75 and multiply by 10. What is the result?

Answer [   ]

13. Ahmed leaves for work at 8am and arrives at work at 9.17am. He then leaves work at 4.57pm and arrives back at home at 6.03pm. How many minutes has Ahmed spent travelling?

Answer [   ]

14. A car travels at 30 km/h for the first hour, 65km/h for the second hour, 44 km/h for the third hour and 50 km/h for the fourth hour. What is the car's average speed over the 4-hour journey?

Answer [   ]

ANSWERS TO NUMERICAL REASONING QUESTIONS – EXERCISE 1

1. £45.56

2. 700

3. 608

4. £150

5. 5

6. 90%

7. 25%

8. 1645 hours or 4.45pm

9. 60 cakes

10. 168

11. 4

12. 1000

13. 143 minutes

14. 47.25 km/h

Now that you have had chance to work through exercise one, try answering the questions that are contained in exercise two. Don't forget to work quickly yet accurately.

how2become

NUMERICAL REASONING QUESTIONS – EXERCISE 2

You are not permitted to use a calculator during this exercise.

There are 20 multiple-choice questions and you have 10 minutes in which to answer them all.

1. Your friends tell you their electricity bill has gone up from £40 per month to £47 per month. How much extra are they now paying per year?

    a. £84   **b.** £85   **c.** £83   **d.** £86   **e.** £82

    Answer [   ]

2. A woman earns a salary of £32,000 per year. How much would she earn in 15 years?

    a. £280,000   **b.** £380,000   **c.** £480,000
    d. £260,000   **e.** £460,000

    Answer [   ]

3. If a police officer walks the beat for 6 hours at a pace of 4km/h, how much ground will she have covered after the 6 hours is over?

    a. 20km   **b.** 21km   **c.** 22km   **d.** 23km   **e.** 24km

    Answer [   ]

4. It takes Malcolm 45 minutes to walk 6 miles to work. At what pace does he walk?

    a. 7 mph   **b.** 4 mph   **c.** 6 mph   **d.** 5 mph   **e.** 8 mph

    Answer

5. Ellie spends 3 hours on the phone talking to her friend abroad. If the call costs 12 pence per 5 minutes, how much does the call cost in total?

    a. £3.30   **b.** £4.32   **c.** £3.32   **d.** £4.44   **e.** £3.44

    Answer

6. A woman spends £27 in a retail store. She has a discount voucher that reduces the total cost to £21.60. How much discount does the voucher give her?

    a. 5%   **b.** 10%   **c.** 15%   **d.** 20%   **e.** 25%

    Answer

7. A group of 7 men spend £21.70 on a round of drinks. How much does each of them pay if the bill is split evenly?

    a. £3.00   **b.** £65.10   **c.** £3.10   **d.** £3.15   **e.** £3.20

    Answer

8. 45,600 people attend a football match to watch Manchester United play Tottenham Hotspur. If there are 32,705 Manchester United supporters at the game, how many Tottenham Hotspur supporters are there?

    a. 12,985   **b.** 13,985   **c.** 12, 895   **d.** 12,895   **e.** 14, 985

    Answer

9. The police are called to attend a motorway accident involving a coach full of passengers. A total of 54 people are on board, 17 of whom are injured. How many are not injured?

    a. 40   **b.** 39   **c.** 38   **d.** 37   **e.** 36

    Answer

10. A car journey usually takes 6 hrs and 55 minutes, but on one occasion the car stops for a total of 47 minutes. How long does the journey take on this occasion?

    a. 6 hrs 40 mins   **b.** 5 hrs 45 mins   **c.** 7 hrs 40 mins
    d. 7 hrs 42 mins   **e.** 6 hrs 42 mins

    Answer

11. There are 10 people in a team. Five of them weigh 70 kg each and the remaining 5 weigh 75 kg each. What is the average weight of the team?

    a. 72.5 kg   **b.** 71.5 kg   **c.** 70.5 kg   **d.** 72 kg   **e.** 71 kg

    Answer

12. A kitchen floor takes 80 tiles to cover. A man buys 10 boxes, each containing 6 tiles. How many more boxes does he need to complete the job?

    a. 2 boxes   **b.** 4 boxes   **c.** 6 boxes
    d. 8 boxes   **e.** 10 boxes

    Answer

13. How much money does it cost to buy 12 packets of crisps at 47 pence each?

    a. £6.45   **b.** £5.64   **c.** £6.54   **d.** £4.65   **e.** £5.46

    Answer

14. A motorcyclist is travelling at 78 mph on a road where the speed limit is 50 mph. How much over the speed limit is he?

    a. 20 mph   **b.** 22 mph   **c.** 26 mph
    d. 28 mph   **e.** 30 mph

    Answer

15. A removal firm loads 34 boxes onto a van. If there are 27 boxes still to be loaded, how many boxes are there in total?

    a. 49   **b.** 50   **c.** 61   **d.** 52   **e.** 53

    Answer

16. When paying a bill at the bank you give the cashier one £20 note, two £5 notes, four £1 coins, six 10p coins and two 2p coins. How much have you given him?

    a. £34.64   **b.** £43.46   **c.** £34.46
    d. £63.44   **e.** £36.46

    Answer [   ]

17. If you pay £97.70 per month on your council tax bill, how much would you pay quarterly?

    a. £293.30   **b.** £293.20   **c.** £293.10
    d. £293.00   **e.** £292.90

    Answer [   ]

18. Four people eat a meal at a restaurant. The total bill comes to £44.80. How much do they need to pay each?

    a. £10.00   **b.** £10.10   **c.** £10.20
    d. £11.10   **e.** £11.20

    Answer [   ]

19. A worker is required to work for 8 hours a day. He is entitled to three 20-minute breaks and one 1-hour lunch break during that 8-hour period. If he works for 5 days per week, how many hours will he have worked after 4 weeks?

    a. 12 hours   **b.** 14 hours   **c.** 120 hours
    d. 140 hours   **e.** 150 hours

    Answer

20. If there are 610 metres in a mile, how many metres are there in 4 miles?

    a. 240   **b.** 2040   **c.** 2044   **d.** 2440   **e.** 244

    Answer

ANSWERS TO NUMERICAL REASONING QUESTIONS – EXERCISE 2

1. a. £84
    In this question you need to first work out the difference in their electricity bill. Subtract £40 from £47 to be left with £7. Now you need to calculate how much extra they are paying per year. If there are 12 months in a year then you need to multiply £7 by 12 months to reach your answer of £84.

2. c. £480,000
    The lady earns £32,000 per year. To work out how much she earns in 15 years, you must multiply £32,000 by 15 years to reach your answer of £480,000.

3. e. 24km
    To work this answer out all you need to do is multiply the 6 hours by the 4 km/h to reach the total of 24 km. Remember that she is walking at a pace of 4 km per hour for a total of 6 hours.

4. e. 8mph
    Malcolm walks 6 miles in 45 minutes, which means he is walking two miles every 15 minutes. Therefore, he would walk 8 miles in 60 minutes (1 hour), so he is walking at 8 mph.

5. b. £4.32
    If the call costs 12 pence for every 5 minutes then all you need to do is calculate how many 5 minutes there are in the 3-hour telephone call. There are 60 minutes in every hour, so therefore there are 180 minutes in 3 hours. 180 minutes divided by 5 minutes will give you 36. To get your answer, just multiply 36 by 12 pence to reach your answer of £4.32

6. d. 20%

   This type of question can be tricky, especially when you don't have a calculator! The best way to work out the answer is to first of all work out how much 10% discount would give you off the total price. If £27 is the total price, then 10% would be a £2.70 discount. In monetary terms the woman has received £5.40 in discount. If 10% is a £2.70 discount then 20% is a £5.40 discount.

7. c. £3.10

   Divide £21.70 by 7 to reach your answer of £3.10.

8. d. 12,895

   Subtract 32,705 from 45,600 to reach your answer of 12,895.

9. d. 37

   Subtract 17 from 54 to reach your answer of 37.

10. d. 7 hrs 42 minutes

    Add the 47 minutes to the normal journey time of 6 hrs and 55 minutes to reach your answer of 7 hrs and 42 minutes.

11. a. 72.5 kg

    To calculate the average weight, you need to first of all add each weight together. Therefore, (5 × 70) + (5 × 75) = 725 kg. To find the average weight you must now divide the 725 by 10, which will give you the answer 72.5 kg.

12. b. 4 boxes

    The man has 10 boxes, each of which contains 6 tiles. He therefore has a total of 60 tiles. He now needs a further 20 tiles to cover the total floor area. If there are 6 tiles in a box then he will need a further 4 boxes (24 tiles).

13. b. £5.64

Multiply 12 by 47 pence to reach your answer of £5.64.

14. d. 28 mph

Subtract 50 mph from 78 mph to reach your answer of 28 mph.

15. c. 61

Add 34 to 27 to reach your answer of 61 boxes.

16. a. £34.64

Add all of the currency together to reach the answer of £34.64.

17. c. £293.10

To reach the answer you must multiply £97.70 by 3. Remember, a quarter is every 3 months.

18. e. £11.20

Divide £44.80 by 4 people to reach your answer of £11.20.

19. c. 120 hours

First of all you need to determine how many 'real' hours he works each day. Subtract the total sum of breaks from 8 hours to reach 6 hours per day. If he works 5 days per week then he is working a total of 30 hours per week. Multiply 30 hours by 4 weeks to reach your answer of 120 hours.

20. d. 2440 metres

Multiply 4 by 610 metres to reach your answer of 2440 metres.

TIPS FOR PASSING THE NUMERICAL REASONING TEST

- Try plenty of sample test questions in the build up to the assessment.

- Try to work without a calculator. This will increase your skill at being able to answer the questions.

- Try to work quickly yet accurately through the test. If you miss a question then make sure you leave a gap on the answer sheet.

- If you generally struggle with this type of test then consider getting a personal tutor.

- During the test do not concentrate on the other candidates and how fast they are working. Keep your head down and focus only on your own performance.

THE WRITTEN EXERCISE – REPORT WRITING

During the assessment centre you may be asked to undertake a written exercise. The written exercise will last for 20 minutes. The assessors will show you into an exercise room and give you a thorough briefing before you start the exercise. They will provide paper and pens, together with a 'proposal document' template to write your response. You will also receive a separate piece of paper, which they will not assess. They will tell you when you have five minutes left and again when you have one minute left.

The assessors will assess the written exercise after you have finished the whole assessment process. In the written exercise you may have to write a proposal document about an issue within a fictitious venue or town. You will not need any prior information or knowledge about policing or further details about fictitious venue or town. All the information you will need to provide an answer will be provided in the candidate preparation material which will be given to you at the assessment process.

In order to help you prepare for the creation of a written report we will now provide you with a fictitious scenario and an explanation of how to approach it.

Please note: the following scenario is not the one that you will be provided with on the day of your assessment. However, the process that we use when creating our report can be used in order to create a sound report.

SAMPLE WRITTEN EXERCISE 1

You are the customer services officer for a fictitious retail centre. Your manager has asked you to compile a report based on a new pub that is being opened in the centre. Your manager is meeting with the pub owners in a few days' time to discuss a few issues and he wants you to write a report based on the information provided. The pub owners have requested that the pub is open to serve alcohol beverages in the centre from 11am until 11pm.

At the bottom of this page there is a survey sheet that tells you that, on the whole, the general public and staff are not happy with the idea of a pub being opened in the shopping centre because of perceived antisocial behavioural problems, littering and rowdiness.

It is your job to create a report for your manager stating what the main issues are and what your recommendations would be.

SURVEY SHEET FOR SAMPLE EXERCISE 1

The following information has been taken from a survey that was conducted amongst 100 members of public who regularly shop at the centre and 30 employees who work at the centre.

- 60% of the general public and 80% of employees felt that the opening of a pub in the centre would increase littering.

- 80% of the general public and 60% of employees thought that rowdiness in the centre would increase as a result of the pub opening.

- 10% of the general public and 10% of employees thought that the opening of the pub would be a good idea.

On the following page there is an example of how the report could be written. There are many different recommendations that could have been made.

You should consider the information you have gathered and make the recommendation(s) you consider to be the best for those circumstances.

Remember: recommendations are suggestions for actions or changes. They should be specific rather than general. It is important that you answer the question and state what your main findings and recommendations are.

SAMPLE RESPONSE TO WRITTEN EXERCISE 1

From: The Customer Services Officer

To: The Centre Manager

Subject: New pub

Sir,

Please find detailed my findings and recommendations in relation to the new pub as requested. The survey conducted took into the consideration the views and opinions of 100 members of the public and 30 members of staff who work at the centre.

Whilst a small proportion of staff and public (10%) felt that the opening of the pub would be a good idea, the majority of people surveyed felt that there would be problems with anti-social behaviour, littering and rowdiness.

Having taken into consideration all of the information provided, I wish to make the following recommendations:

The level of customer service that the centre currently provides is high and it is important that this is maintained. It is important to take into consideration the views and opinions of our customers and staff and to see things from their point of view. I believe that there would be a high risk involved if we were to allow the pub to serve alcoholic beverages from 11am until 11pm and that problems with anti-social behaviour could develop. We have a responsibility to protect the public and to ensure that they are safe whilst in the centre.

Whilst it is important to initially obtain the views of the pub owners, I recommend that the pub is only permitted to serve alcoholic beverages from 11am until 1pm and from 5pm until 7pm so as to reduce the risk of the above problems developing.

I have recommended this course of action, as I believe it is in the best interests of the centre, its staff and more importantly our valued customers. This alternative course of action would be for a trial period only and providing there are no problems with anti-social behaviour, littering or rowdiness we could look to review the opening hours with a view to extending them. I am prepared to take full responsibility for monitoring the situation once the pub has been opened. I will keep you updated on progress.

THE CUSTOMER SERVICES OFFICER

Now that you have read the sample response, take a look at the following 5 step approach that we use when creating a well structured report.

HOW TO CREATE AN EFFECTIVE REPORT – THE 5 STEP APPROACH

STEP 1
Read the information provided in the exercise quickly and accurately
Remember that you only have 20 minutes in which to create your report. Therefore, you do not want to spend too long reading the information. We would suggest that you spend 2-3 minutes maximum reading the information.

STEP 2
Extract relevant information from irrelevant information (main findings)
When you read the information provided in the exercise you will notice that some of the information is of no significance. Write down which information is relevant in brief details only – these should be your main findings.

STEP 3
Decide what recommendations you are going to suggest or what action(s) you are going to take
One of the core competencies is that of problem solving. If asked to, then you must come up with suitable recommendations. Do not 'sit on the fence', but rather provide a logical solution to the problem.

STEP 4
Construct your report in a logical and concise manner
You are being assessed on your ability to communicate effectively. Therefore you must construct your report in a logical and concise manner. You must also ensure that you answer the question.

STEP 5
Include keywords and phrases from the core competencies in your report
During each report or letter that you construct we strongly advise that you include keywords and phrases from the core competencies.

You will notice that the 5 step approach is easy to follow. Therefore, we strongly suggest that you learn it and use it during the practise exercises provided later on in this section.

To begin with, let's go back to the sample response that we provided to the first exercise and we will explain how to implement the 5 step approach.

Step 1 requires you to read the information quickly and accurately.

Step 2 requires you to extract relevant information from irrelevant information. In order to demonstrate what is relevant we have underlined the key points.

SAMPLE EXERCISE 1

You are the customer services officer for a fictitious retail centre. Your manager has asked you to compile a report based on a **new pub that is being opened in the centre**.

Your manager is meeting with the pub owners in a few days time to discuss a few issues and he wants you to write a report based on the information provided. **The pub owners have requested that the pub is open to serve alcohol beverages in the centre from 11am until 11pm**.

On the following page a survey sheet is provided, which tells you that, on the whole, **the general public and staff are not happy with the idea of a pub being opened in the shopping centre** because of perceived antisocial behavioural problems, littering and rowdiness.

It is your job to create a report **stating what your main findings are** and what **your recommendations would be**.

SURVEY SHEET

The following information has been taken from a survey that was conducted amongst 100 members of the public who regularly shop at the centre and 30 employees who work at the centre.

- 60% of the general public and 80% of employees felt that the opening of a pub in the centre would increase littering.

- 80% of the general public and 60% of employees thought that rowdiness in the centre would increase as a result of the pub opening.

- 10% of the general public and 10% of employees thought that the opening of the pub would be a good idea.

So, why are the key points that we underlined relevant? Allow us to explain:

You are the customer services officer
Because you are a customer services officer it is important that you provide a high level of service. Therefore, the report that you create needs to cater for everyone's needs. In relation to this particular situation you must provide a solution that caters for the needs of the pub owners, the centre and also the members of public and employees.

New pub that is being opened in the centre.
The information you have been provided with tells you clearly that a new pub is opening in the centre. Therefore, the pub needs to operate as a business and by doing so it needs to serve alcoholic beverages. Despite that fact that the majority of people surveyed are against the pub opening, the pub still needs to function as a business. Bear this in mind when detailing your recommendations.

The pub owners have requested that the pub is open to serve alcohol beverages in the centre from 11am until 11pm
The pub owners have quite rightly requested that the opens from 11am until 11pm and serves alcoholic beverages during this period. However, you still need to provide a high level of service to everyone. Therefore, you may decide to recommend a reduced opening time for a trial period only. Always look for the obvious solution to the problem.

The general public and staff are not happy with the idea of a pub being opened in the shopping centre
Because the general public and staff are not happy with the idea of a pub opening in the centre you will need to take this into account when constructing your response.

Stating what your main findings are

Your first task when writing your report is to do just that – state what your main findings are.

Your recommendations would be

Once you have detailed the main issues you will then need to make your recommendations which should be based on sound judgement and common sense.

During step 3 you will need to come up with your recommendations. Remember that as a Police Special Constable you will need to solve problems based on the information and facts provided. In this particular case we have decided to offer a solution that meets the needs of all parties' concerned – reduced opening times for a trial period with a view to extending them if all goes well. When creating your report do not be afraid to come up with sensible recommendations or solutions.

During step 4 you will create your report. It is important that your report is concise, relevant and that it flows in a logical sequence. We would strongly recommend that you construct it using the following format:

Beginning

During the introduction provide brief details as to what the report is about. You should also provide brief details that relate to your findings. In this particular question we are being asked to detail our main findings and recommendations. Therefore we will detail our main findings during the beginning section of the report.

Middle

Here you will write your main findings and recommendations. Remember to include keywords and phrases that you have learnt from the core competencies.

End

This is the summary and conclusion. Say why you have recommended this course of action. Are there any further recommendations? If you are expecting there to be feedback, explain how you propose to deal with this. You may also wish to state that you will take full responsibility for seeing any action through and for keeping your manager updated on progress.

In order to demonstrate how effective the beginning, middle and end method can be we have boxed off each section on the following page.

Creating a report using a beginning, middle and an end

Sir,

Please find detailed my findings and recommendations in relation to the new pub as requested. The survey conducted took into the consideration the views and opinions of 100 members of the public and 30 members of staff who work at the centre.

Whilst a small proportion of staff and public (10%) felt that the opening of the pub would be a good idea, the majority of people surveyed felt that there would be problems with anti-social behaviour, littering and rowdiness.

Having taken into consideration all of the information provided, I wish to make the following recommendations:

The level of customer service that the centre currently provides is high and it is important that this is maintained. It is important to take into consideration the views and opinions of our customers and staff and to see things from their point of view. I believe that there would be a high risk involved if we were to allow the pub to serve alcoholic beverages from 11am until 11pm and that problems with anti-social behaviour could develop. We have a responsibility to protect the public and to ensure that they are safe whilst in the centre.

Whilst it is important to initially obtain the views of the pub owners, I recommend that the pub is only permitted to serve alcoholic beverages from 11am until 1pm and from 5pm until 7pm so as to reduce the risk of the above problems developing.

I have recommended this course of action, as I believe it is in the best interests of the centre, its staff and more importantly our valued customers. This alternative course of action would be for a trial period only and providing there are no problems with anti-social behaviour, littering or rowdiness we could look to review the opening hours with a view to extending them. I am prepared to take full responsibility for monitoring the situation once the pub has been opened. I will keep you updated on progress.

The Customer Services Officer

The final step in creating your report is to use keywords and phrases when writing your response which are relevant to the core competencies being assessed. The following are sentences and phrases that we used whilst creating our report that relate to a number of competency areas:

1. "The level of customer service that the centre currently provides is high and it is important that this is maintained" – **relates to community and customer focus.**

2. "It is important to take into consideration the views and opinions of our customers and staff and to see things from their point of view" – **relates to respect for race and diversity.**

3. "I believe that there would be a high risk involved if we were to allow the pub to serve alcoholic beverages from 11am until 11pm and that problems with anti-social behaviour could develop" – **relates to problem solving and resilience.**

4. "We have a responsibility to protect the public and to ensure that they are safe whilst in the centre" – **relates to personal responsibility.**

5. "Whilst it is important to initially obtain the views of the pub owners, I recommend that the pub is only permitted to serve alcoholic beverages from 11am until 1pm and from 5pm until 7pm so as to reduce the risk of the above problems developing" – **relates to respect for race and diversity and also problem solving.**

6. "I have recommended this course of action, as I believe it is in the best interests of the centre, its staff and more importantly our valued customers" – **relates to customer focus.**

7. "This alternative course of action would be for a trial period only and providing there are no problems with anti-social behaviour, littering or rowdiness we could look to review the opening hours with a view to extending them" – **relates to problem solving and resilience.**

8. "I am prepared to take full responsibility for monitoring the situation once the pub has been opened" – **relates to personal responsibility.**

9. "I will keep you updated on progress" – **relates to teamworking.**

You will now see how important it is to learn the core competencies before you attend the assessment centre.

Before you have a go yourself at a number of report writing exercises we will provide you with some final hints and tips on how to create an effective report.

IMPORTANT TIPS TO HELP YOU STRUCTURE A GOOD REPORT

- Remember that you are being assessed against effective communication. This means creating a report that concise, relevant and easy to read.

- Make sure you **answer** the question.

- Aim to make zero grammar, spelling or punctuation errors. If you are unsure about a word, do not use it.

- Create your report using a beginning, middle and an end as we have suggested.

- Use keywords and phrases from the core competencies. This is how the police will assess you.

- Do not spend too much time reading the information and documentation provided. Spend a maximum of 3 minutes reading and digesting the documentation, and then spend at least 15 minutes writing your report. The final 2 minutes can be used for checking your report for errors.

Now that you know how to create a written report, try the sample exercises on the following pages. We have provided you with a template following each exercise for you to create your report. Don't forget to have a copy of the core competencies next to you when writing your practice reports.

WRITTEN REPORT SAMPLE EXERCISE 2

You are the customer services officer for a fictitious retail centre based in Sandford Town. Your manager has asked you to compile a report regarding a number of complaints he has received from shop owners who state that rowdy youths are intimidating shop owners at the centre which is having a detrimental effect on their business generally and more importantly their takings. Visitor numbers at the centre are down 25% over the last 3 months.

CCTV reports suggest that a gang of 8 youths have been circling the centre during daylight shopping hours, often approaching customers and harassing them for spare change.

The local newspaper have become aware of these incidents and they are sending a reporter along to interview your manager to see what the main problems are and what the centre intends to do about them.

Your report should detail your main findings and also your recommendations as to how the situation can be resolved and what your manager should say to the reporter when he meets him.

Use the template on the following page to create your response.

Written report sample exercise 2 template

From:

To:

Title:

WRITTEN REPORT SAMPLE EXERCISE 3

You are the customer services officer for a fictitious retail centre. Your manager has received a request from the local council Anti Truancy Group who wish to patrol the centre in groups of 6 people for five day period next month.

During their request the Anti Truancy Group has raised concerns that school children from the local area are congregating at the retail centre during school hours. CCTV cameras have confirmed these reports.

Local police have also confirmed in a recent report that anti social behaviour in the area of the retail centre has increased by 15% in the last four weeks alone.

You are to create report for your manager that details your main findings and your recommendations for solving the problem.

Use the template on the following page to create your response.

Written report sample exercise 3 template

From:

To:

Title:

THE SITUATION JUDGEMENT TEST

The Situational Judgment Test is a multiple-choice test based on common situations that you may come across as a Special Constable.

During the actual SJT assessment you will be required to answer 50 questions within a 65 minute time-frame.

Take a look at the following sample SJT question:

Sample Situational Judgement Test question 1

Whilst on foot patrol in your local High Street you are approached by a woman who informs you that she has just found a purse on the pavement. Upon inspection there is no money in the purse but you do notice personal details relating to the owner.

Please pick the best option (most effective option) and the worst option (least effective option) in terms of what you should do:

A. Challenge the woman as to why there is no money in the purse.

B. Immediately take the purse back to the station and record the lost property.

C. Ask the woman to hand the purse in at the local police station.

D. Immediately try to contact the owner of the purse in order to hand it back to them.

Answers

BEST OPTION: D

This option allows you to reunite the owner with the purse quickly and also allows you to stay out on patrol.

WORST OPTION: A

This option could potentially damage relations with the public. You have no reason to suspect the woman has taken money from the purse.

Now take a look at the next sample question.

Sample Situational Judgement Test question 2

It is 2200hrs and you are on duty at a music festival. You have not had a break for eight hours and you are feeling very tired and hungry. The festival is very busy and the revellers have been drinking heavily. There is potential for disruption. All other units in the area are busy as it is a Saturday evening and there is nobody to discuss the situation with face to face. There is a mobile food unit at the entrance to the festival where you could discretely take a well-earned break without many people noticing.

Please pick the best option (most effective option) and the worst option (least effective option) in terms of what you should do:

A. Take a break at the mobile food unit and leave your post without anyone knowing. After all, you deserve a rest.

B. Work through your tiredness and hunger and maintain position at your post.

C. Contact your Police Sergeant by radio and inform him/her that you have not had a break for eight hours and request a relief.

D. Buy a takeaway cup of tea and some food and eat it at your post.

Answers

BEST OPTION: C

You must contact your Police sergeant or supervisor and inform them that you need a break. If you are tired and hungry then you are unlikely to perform to the best of your ability.

WORST OPTION: A

This could lead to potential disorder with nobody being aware that assistance is needed in the area at the festival.

You will notice that you need no prior knowledge of police procedures in order to answer the questions. All you need is a good level of sensible thinking.

During the next section we have provided you with 10 test question to help you prepare. Work through the questions carefully and learn as you progress. Do not worry if you get some questions wrong. This is all part of the learning process and is only natural. The important thing is to learn from your mistakes and to understand how the answers are reached.

IO SAMPLE SITUATIONAL JUDGEMENT TEST QUESTIONS

SAMPLE QUESTION 1

A work colleague at your station has been absent due to sickness and she has missed an important operational incident debrief that has highlighted a number of important change to police procedures. What would you do?

Please pick the best option (most effective option) and the worst option (least effective option) in terms of what you should do.

A. Immediately explain to her what the changes are and clarify that she fully understands them.

B. Inform your line manager of her absence so that he can tell her what they are.

C. Do nothing. She will probably find out about the changes through other work colleagues or whilst she is on the job.

D. Wait until tea break before you inform her. There'll be more time then to explain what the changes are.

Notes

SAMPLE QUESTION 2

Whilst attending a Road Traffic Collision you notice a member of the public trying to help out the Firefighters by handing them items of equipment. What would you do?

Please pick the best option (most effective option) and the worst option (least effective option) in terms of what you should do.

A. Allow them to carry on as they probably know what they are doing.

B. Approach the person and offer to help them pass over the equipment.

C. Politely thank the person for their assistance but ask them to stay back behind the cordon where they will be safe.

D. Ask your supervisory officer what they think you should do.

Notes

SAMPLE QUESTION 3

Special Constables are often required to enter people's homes in order to carry out door to door enquiries. Whilst attending someone's home they offer you £50 as a thank you for the good work that you do. What would you do?

Please pick the best option (most effective option) and the worst option (least effective option) in terms of what you should do.

A. Thank them for the money, put it in my pocket, and leave a happy person.

B. Thank them for the money, put it in my pocket, and share it with the rest of the team when I get back to the police station.

C. Thank them for their kind offer but explain that you are unable to accept gifts of this nature.

D. Walk away and ignore them.

Notes

SAMPLE QUESTION 4

During an operational incident the Police Sergeant gives you instructions to immediately stop what you are doing and request more resources via the control centre. Once you have received the instructions, what would you do?

Please pick the best option (most effective option) and the worst option (least effective option) in terms of what you should do.

A. Finish off the job that I am doing before contacting the control centre to request more resources.

B. Immediately stop what I am doing if safe to do so before contacting the control centre to request more resources. Once I have requested the resources, and confirmed that the control centre fully understands my request, I will then inform the Sergeant that the message has been sent and that the resources are on their way. I would then return to my previous task.

C. Because I am already involved in another task, I will pass the message onto another Police Officer so that he/she can request the resources.

D. Immediately stop what I am doing if safe to do so before contacting the control centre to request more resources. Once I have requested the resources, and confirmed that the control centre fully understands my request, I will then go back to what I was doing before.

Notes

SAMPLE QUESTION 5

You are the first on the scene of a fire in a block of flats. Which of the following tasks would you carry out first?

Please pick the best option (most effective option) and the worst option (least effective option) in terms of what you should do.

A.   Look for fire extinguishers.

B.   Fight the fire.

C.   Search the building for casualties.

D.   Raise the fire alarm in order to start the evacuation process and then contact the control centre to ask for the attendance of the Fire Service and more police resources.

Notes

SAMPLE QUESTION 6

Whilst patrolling the streets a man runs up to you and tells you that a bank around the corner is in the process of being robbed by an armed gang. Which of the following would you do?

Please pick the best option (most effective option) and the worst option (least effective option) in terms of what you should do.

A. Ask the man to take you to the shop where the robbery is taking place. Once you get there you can decide what action to take.

B. Immediately contact control to inform them of the location of incident and the circumstances surrounding it, i.e. that the robbers are armed. This will enable the control centre to deploy the correct resources.

C. Gather as much information from the man as possible about the incident and its location before making your way to the scene.

D. Immediately run to the location of the robbery and attempt to tackle the armed robbers.

Notes

SAMPLE QUESTION 7

You are responsible for the outer cordon at a serious incident when a man approaches you saying that he is from the local press and that he wants to take some pictures of the incident from within the inner cordon. What would you do?

Please pick the best option (most effective option) and the worst option (least effective option) in terms of what you should do.

A. Allow him into the inner cordon.

B. Tell him to go away.

C. Politely inform him that he is not permitted within the inner cordon and ask him respectfully to stay back away from the danger area.

D. Ask your supervisor what he/she thinks you should do.

Notes

SAMPLE QUESTION 8

During a visit to a local school you notice that a number of the fire doors are wedged open illegally. What would you do?

Please pick the best option (most effective option) and the worst option (least effective option) in terms of what you should do.

A.   Ignore it for the time being. You are at the school on a talk and it would be inappropriate to say anything there and then.

B.   Report the situation to the local Fire Safety Officer when you return to the police station.

C.   Inform the school Head teacher that he/she must remove the wedges immediately.

D.   Inform the school Head teacher that he/she must remove the wedges immediately and explain why the fire doors must not be wedged open. In addition to this I would inform the local Fire Safety Officer upon returning to the police station so that he/she could carry out an inspection of the school.

Notes

SAMPLE QUESTION 9

You are attending an incident that involves anti-social behaviour when an elderly woman approaches you and tells you that there is another similar incident a few roads away. What would you do?

Please pick the best option (most effective option) and the worst option (least effective option) in terms of what you should do.

A.   Quickly make my way to the new incident.

B.   Immediately take further details from the woman before radioing police control to inform them of the new incident so that another patrol can make their way there.

C.   Ignore it. The lady has probably mistaken the two incidents as the same one.

D.   Ask your line manager what they think you should do.

Notes

SAMPLE QUESTION 10

You are attending a crime scene and your supervisory officer and asked you to stand by the entrance to the building and not allow anyone to enter without her permission. It is important that the crime scene is preserved whilst they await the attendance of forensics. A regular Police Officer walks up to you and says he needs to enter the building. What do you do?

Please pick the best option (most effective option) and the worst option (least effective option) in terms of what you should do.

A.   Let him enter.

B.   Ask him to wait outside whilst you contact your supervisory officer by radio to ask for permission for him to enter.

C.   Tell him to leave. Nobody is allowed to enter under any circumstances.

D.   Check his identification before allowing him to enter.

Notes

Now that you have completed the test, please work through the following answers carefully, For any that you have scored incorrectly, take the time o read the explanations as this will help you to improve for the real test.

ANSWERS TO SITUATIONAL JUDGEMENT TEST

QUESTION 1
BEST: A
It is important that all members of staff are kept up-to-date with issues that affect their role. It is good practice to inform your colleague of details of the meeting that she missed.

WORST: C
This option is not taking responsibility and is poor practice. You should never assume that your colleague will find out the information from someone else. Take action yourself and inform them of the information.

QUESTION 2
BEST: C
Although the member of public is trying to help, there is a danger they could become injured whilst handling the equipment. Health and safety rules and regulations dictate that this kind of practice should not be permitted.

WORST: A or B
Either of these responses would be the worst. By helping the person you would be condoning their actions. By ignoring it, you would also be condoning it.

QUESTION 3

BEST: C

You are not permitted to accept gifts of any nature whilst on duty or otherwise for working as a police special constable. Politely refusing is the best option.

WORST: A or B

You must never accept gifts of any description for your work in a public office.

QUESTION 4

BEST: B

This is clearly the most effective option. Not only are you carrying out a direct order but you are also confirming with the control centre that they have received the message and you are also confirming with the Police Sergeant that you have carried out the request successfully.

WORST: A

The danger with this option is that you might forget to send the message once you have completed the task. In addition to this you are failing to carry out a direct order by a senior officer by not 'immediately' stopping what you are doing in order to carry out the requested task.

QUESTION 5

BEST: D

In any incident of this nature you need to raise the alarm in order to start the evacuation process. You must then make provision for the relevant services and backup to be deployed.

WORST: B

If you start an attempt to fight the fire, without either raising the alarm or using the correct personal protective equipment, then you will be placing your life and the lives of others in danger.

QUESTION 6

BEST: B

During an incident of this nature it is imperative that the correct resources are deployed. If the robbers are armed then the lives could be in serious danger. Therefore, it is imperative that the control centre is informed so that the relevant response can be deployed.

WORST: D

Running to the incident, without sufficient information and resources, could place lives in danger.

QUESTION 7

BEST: C

Part of the role of a police special constable involves providing excellent customer service. Therefore, you should be polite to the individual, but inform them that it is not possible for him to enter.

WORST: A

You should never allow anyone into the inner cordon of an incident without the permission of the officer-in-charge. This is primarily for health and safety reasons.

QUESTION 8

BEST: D

The correct answer here is to inform the school Head teacher that he/she must remove the wedges immediately. This will hopefully reduce any risk of fire spread in the case of a fire. You should also take the opportunity to educate them and explain why the fire doors must not be wedged open. You should also follow up your actions by informing the local Fire Safety Officer upon returning to the police station so that he/she could carry out an inspection of the school, just in case there are any further contraventions.

WORST: A

The worst thing you can do is ignore it. You have a duty of care whilst at the school and therefore you should take action immediately.

QUESTION 9

BEST: B

Whilst attending the first incident you have a duty of care; therefore, you should stay at the scene unless the other incident involves a danger to life. The correct answer is to inform the control centre so that they can deploy the relevant response.

WORST: C

You must never ignore a report of an incident.

QUESTION 10

BEST: B

Although he is a serving police officer you have been told not to let anyone into the crime scene area; therefore, you should obey the instruction. The best option is to inform the officer-in-charge of the request to enter so that they can decide on the best course of action.

WORST: A

By allowing the officer to enter you are effectively disobeying a direct order.

THE ROLE-PLAY/INTERACTIVE EXERCISES

During the assessment centre you may have to deal with a number of interactive exercises or role plays as they are otherwise called. Not all police forces are requiring Police Special Constable applicants to undergo this assessment, so we advise that you confirm if you are required to undertake this particular element before reading on.

The type of situation that you will be confronted with varies greatly. However, examples of the types of exercises that have been used in the past include the following:

- A manager of a store that is inside a fictitious retail centre wants to discuss an issue with you that relates to the lack of security.

- A customer who has been shopping at a fictitious retail centre wants to talk to you about a conversation they have had with another customer.

- A school teacher who has been visiting the retail centre would like to discuss an issue with you regarding his/her pupils.

- A member of staff who works at the fictitious retail centre would like to discuss an issue with you.

The situation that you will have to deal with is irrelevant. It is how you interact with the role play actor and what you say that is important. You must be able to demonstrate the core competencies during each role-play scenario. Examples of how you would achieve this include:

- Dealing with the role play actor in a sensitive and supportive manner;

- Having respect for people's views and feelings;

- Seeing issues from others' points of view;

- Ask relevant questions to clarify the situation;

- Listening to people's needs and interests;

- Respecting confidentiality where appropriate;

- Presenting an appropriate image;

- Trying to sort out customers' problems as soon as possible;

- Make reference to any supporting documentation, policies or procedures;

- Confirming that the customer is happy with your offered solution.

- Keeping customers updated on any progress that you make.

It is crucial that you learn the core competencies and are also able to demonstrate them during each exercise.

This part of the selection process will normally be split into two five-minute parts. The first part will consist of the preparation phase and the second part will be the actual activity phase that you'll be assessed against. We will now explain each phase in detail.

THE PREPARATION PHASE

During the five-minute preparation phase you will be provided with the actual scenario, either on a card or sheet of paper. You may also be provided with additional documentation that is relevant to the scenario that you'll be required to deal with. You will be taken to a desk or a separate room where you

will have just five minutes in which to prepare for the activity phase. During the preparation phase you will be allowed to take notes and then use them during the activity phase. At the end of the activity phase you will normally be required to hand in your notes to the assessor. You will not be permitted to take any writing utensils into the activity phase. Although the preparation phase is not assessable, you must still use the time wisely. This is how we recommend you use the time:

- Quickly read the scenario and any supporting information/documentation.

- Once you have studied the scenario and any additional information/documentation you should then separate relevant information from irrelevant information, just like you did during the written report writing stage. Write down brief notes as to what you think is relevant.

- You now need to cross match any relevant information from the scenario with procedures, policies and your responsibilities that are provided in the information provided. For example, if within the scenario it becomes apparent that somebody from the centre is being bullied or harassed, you will need to know, use and make reference to any equality policy statement that is available during the activity phase of the assessment. Another example would be where a child has been reported missing. If this was the case then you would possibly wish to make use of the security guards, the tannoy system and also the CCTV cameras that are based around the centre, if this information is provided.

- We would now recommend that you write down on your note paper a step-by-step approach as what you intend to do during the activity stage. An example of this may be as follows:

STEP 1
Introduce myself to the role actor and
ask him/her how I can help them.
(Remember to be polite and respectful and treat the role
play actor in a sensitive and supportive manner. You are
being assessed against the core competency of respect for
race and diversity during every role play scenario)

STEP 2
Listen to them carefully and ask relevant questions
to establish the facts.
(How, When, Where, Why, Who)

STEP 3
Clarify the information received to check you have
understood exactly what has happened.

STEP 4

Provide a suitable solution to the problem or situation
and tell the role play actor what you intend to do.
(Remember to use keywords and phrases
from the core competencies)

STEP 5
Check to confirm that the role play actor is happy with your solution.
Provide a final summary of what you intend to do and ask them
if there is anything else you can help them with.
(Tell the role actor that you will take personal
responsibility for solving the problem and that you
will keep them updated on progress)

Once you have made your notes and created a plan of action
you are now ready to go through to the activity phase. Before
we move on to this stage of the role play assessment we will
provide you with a further explanation of how you may wish
to approach the preparation phase using a sample scenario.

SAMPLE ROLE-PLAY EXERCISE 1

You are the customer service manager at a fictitious retail centre. A member of your staff approaches you and tells you that she has been bullied by another member of staff. The woman is clearly upset by the situation and she wants you to take action.

How to prepare

Study any supporting information that is available to you and in particular any details of an equality policy statement. If there is such a statement you will find specific details about how to deal with situations of this nature and it is essential that you follow each step carefully. Remember that one of the assessable core competencies requires you to follow and refer to policies and procedures.

Using your 5-step plan the following is how you might deal with this type of situation:

STEP 1 – Walk into the activity room and introduce yourself to the role actor. Ask them sensitively what the problem was and how you can help them. If there was a chair available in the room then ask them if they would like to sit down.

STEP 2 – Listen very carefully to what they have to say (effective communication) and sympathise where appropriate. Then, start to establish the facts of the case asking them relevant questions such as:

- How long had the bullying been going on for?

- Who was involved and what had they been doing/ saying?

- Were any other people involved?

- Have there been any witnesses to this incident?

- Had they asked the other person to stop bullying them and if so what was their reaction?

STEP 3 – Clarify and confirm with the role actor that you have gathered the correct facts.

STEP 4 – At this stage take full control of the situation and tell the role actor what you intend to do about the situation. Make reference at this stage to the equality policy statement and use it as a basis for solving the problem. Use keywords and phrases that match the core competencies.

STEP 5 – During the final stages of the role play activity stage check to confirm that the role play actor is happy with your solution. Provide them with a final summary of what you intend to do and ask them if there is anything else that you can help them with. Also confirm at this stage that you are going to take personal responsibility for resolving the problem and that you will keep them updated on progress as and when it occurred.

Once the 5 minute preparation phase is complete a buzzer will sound and you will then move to the activity stage of the assessment.

The activity phase

The activity stage will again last for 5 minutes and it is during this phase that you are required to interact with the role actor.

During the activity stage there will be an assessor in the room whose responsibility it is to assess you against the core competencies. Try to ignore them and concentrate fully on how you interact with the role actor. There may also be a third person in the room who will be there to shadow the assessor or for quality assurance purposes. During the activity stage you will be assessed on what you did and how you did it.

You will usually be graded from A to D with the highest score earning you an A to the weakest score earning you a D.

Obviously you want to aim for an A but don't be disheartened if you feel that you haven't done well on a particular exercise, as you can make up your grades in another. If you score a D against the core competency of respect for race and diversity then you may fail the entire assessment.

During the previous sample role play exercise (exercise 1) we focused on a complaint made by a member of staff who claimed that she was being bullied by another member of staff. Within the equality policy statement you will find suggested courses of action. The options here may suggest that the person asks the offender to stop, the problem is discussed with an appropriate person (you) or the option is available to make a formal complaint.

Below we have provided you with some suggested responses to this type of exercise followed by an explanation. Most of these can be applied to similar exercises surrounding harassment cases, although you should judge every situation separately and act according to the brief.

SAMPLE RESPONSES AND ACTIONS TO EXERCISE 1

Response
"Thank you for coming to see me today. I understand that you have a problem with another member of staff?"

Explanation
During this type of response you are demonstrating a level of customer care and you are focusing on the needs of the individual. Remember to use open body language and never become confrontational, defensive or aggressive.

Response

"Would you be able to tell me exactly what has happened and how this has affected you? I will also need to ask you whose been bullying you, where it has been occurring and on how many occasions including dates and times."

Explanation

Again you are focusing on the needs of the individual, which is important. Try to look and sound genuine and also use suitable facial expressions. In order to 'problem solve' you must first ask questions and gather the facts of the incident.

Response

"It must be very difficult for you to bring this matter to my attention; you are to be praised for this course of action."

Explanation

During this response you are demonstrating a caring nature and you are providing a high level of service.

Response

"Have you asked him to stop or have you informed anybody else of this situation?"

and

"Are you aware of this happening to anybody else?"

Explanation

Here you are gathering the facts, which will help you provide a suitable resolution to the problem.

Response

"The company equality policy in relation to this kind of alleged behaviour is quite clear, it states XYZ. It will NOT be tolerated and I can assure you the matter will be dealt with."

Explanation

During this response you are detailing the company equality policy. This demonstrates to the assessor that you are fully aware of the policies and procedures – this will gain you higher scores. You are also stating that this type of behaviour is not accepted and you are, therefore, challenging the inappropriate behaviour in line with the police officer core competencies.

Response

"Before I detail my solution to this problem I want to first of all confirm the details of the case. Please can you confirm that...."

Explanation

During this response you are confirming and checking that the details you have obtained are correct.

Response

"Please be aware that you can make a formal complaint if you so wish? Your feelings and wishes are paramount during my investigation. What would you like to happen from here? Would you like to make a formal complaint against the individual concerned?"

Explanation

By asking the complainant what they want to do, you are demonstrating that you are putting their needs first and you are respecting confidentiality.

Response

"Let me assure you that this matter will be dealt with as a priority but in the meantime I will place another member of staff with

you so that you can work in a comfortable environment. Are you happy with this course of action?"

Explanation

Here you are taking action to resolve the problem. You are also informing the person how you intend to resolve it. Finally you are checking that the person is happy with your actions.

Response

"May I thank you again for bringing this matter to my attention; I will keep you fully informed of all progress. I wish to inform you that I will be taking personal responsibility for resolving this issue. Is there anything else I can do for you?"

Explanation

Finally you are demonstrating a high level of customer service and also checking if there is anything else that you can do for them. You are also taking personal responsibility for resolving the issue. It is important to tell them that you will keep them informed of the outcome of any investigation.

TOP TIPS FOR PREPARING FOR THE ROLE-PLAY EXERCISES

- Learn the core competencies that are being assessed and be able to 'act' out each one.

- A good way to practise for these exercises is to get a friend or family relative to 'role-play' the sample exercises contained within this guide.

- When practising the exercises, try to pick someone you know who will make it difficult for you. Also, try to resolve each issue in a calm but effective manner, in line with the core competencies.

 how2become

- You may wish to purchase a copy of the 'Police Role Play' DVD now available at www.how2become.co.uk.

TOP TIPS FOR PASSING FOR THE ROLE-PLAY EXERCISES

- Use the preparation time wisely.

- Learn the pre assessment material before you go to the assessment. This will make your life much easier.

- Remain calm during every role-play. Even if the actor becomes confrontational, it is essential that you remain calm.

- If at any time during the role play activity phase the role play actor uses language that is either inappropriate (including swearing), discriminatory or uses any form of harassment then you must challenge it immediately. When challenging this kind of behaviour you must do so in an assertive manner without becoming aggressive. Always be polite and respectful at all times.

- Use effective listening skills during the role-play exercises and ask questions in order to gather the facts.

- Once you have gathered the facts of the case or situation then solve the problem.

On the following pages we have provided you with two more sample role-play exercises. To begin with, read each exercise carefully and then take notes in the box provided detailing how you might deal with the situation. Make sure you have a copy of the core competencies to hand when making your notes.

Next, get a friend or relative to act out each scenario so you can practise dealing with it.

SAMPLE ROLE-PLAY EXERCISE 2

You are the customer services officer at a fictitious retail centre. A school teacher has lost a pupil in the shopping centre and he wants to discuss the matter with you. He is very annoyed that it took him so long to find your office. He states that there were no security staff around and his pupil has now been missing for fifteen minutes.

He wants to know what you intend to do about it.

How to prepare and possible actions

- To begin with, you should study any information about the centre, if available. What does it say that possibly relates to the above scenario? Is there any CCTV?

- Are there any security staff that could help look for any missing persons?

- Is there a police station within the complex and can the police be used to respond to situations like this?

- Request the attendance of the police immediately.

- Make sure that you keep the teacher in the office with you so that they can provide further information to the police about the missing child.

- Try to gather information about the missing child – How old are they? What are they wearing? What is their name? Are there any distinguishing features? Where were they last seen?

- Try to reassure the teacher that everything will be ok.

- If there is the option of using a loudspeaker system in the shopping centre then this could be used to transmit a 'missing persons' message.

- Consider the option of using the centre's CCTV cameras to locate the missing person.

- Consider positioning a member of the security team at each exit to prevent anybody walking out with the child.

Below we have provided a sample response to this exercise. Read it before using the box on the following page to take notes on how you would deal with this situation.

SAMPLE RESPONSES AND ACTIONS TO EXERCISE 2

"Hello sir, my name is Richard and I'm the customer service manager for this centre. I understand that one of your pupils has gone missing in the centre – is that correct?" (Establish exactly what has happened).

"Firstly can I reassure you that the police have been called and they are on their way. I have also put a security guard at each exit to look out for the missing child. In the meantime I would like to take some notes from you. Please can you give me a full description of the missing pupil please including their name?" (Make a list of the description.)

"Please can you tell me how long ago they have been missing for and where they were last seen?"

"Have you or anybody else been looking for the missing person and have you reported this to anybody else yet?"

"Is there a possibility that they might have wandered off to their favourite shop or gone somewhere else with another parent who was in the group?"

"Do you think they would understand their own name if we broadcast this over the loudspeaker system?"

"OK Sir, thank you for providing me with these details. This is what I propose to do in order to resolve the situation. To begin with I will check the CCTV cameras to see if we can locate the missing child. I will also brief all members of staff at the centre, including the security guards, of the missing child's description. I will also put out a tannoy announcement asking the missing child to go to the nearest customer services desk where a member of staff will meet them."

"In addition to this course of action I will also put the registered nurse on standby so that she can treat the child for shock if appropriate."

"In the meantime please stay here until the police arrive, as it is important you provide them with more information. Let me reassure you that we will do everything we possibly can to locate the missing person. I will be taking personal responsibility for resolving this issue and I will keep you updated on progress as and when it occurs."

Notes for sample role-play exercise 2

SAMPLE ROLE-PLAY EXERCISE 3

You are the customer services officer at a fictitious retail centre. One of the centre store managers wants to see you about a gang of youths who are standing outside his shop behaving in an anti-social manner, swearing and obstructing customers from entering his shop. He is very annoyed at the situation and is losing money because potential customers are not allowed to shop in comfort without feeling threatened.

How to prepare and possible actions

- To begin with you should study the additional information provided to see if any of it is relevant to the scenario. What does the information say that possibly relates to the above scenario? Is this kind of behaviour tolerated? Can people who behave in such a manner be escorted from the centre and should the police be involved? Can you involve the security staff or use the CCTV cameras to provide the police with evidence?

- Remember that the manager is annoyed at the situation and therefore you may have to diffuse a confrontational situation in the first instance. Remember to be firm but stay calm and never become confrontational yourself.

- On the following page we have provided a sample response to this exercise. Read it before using the box on the following page to take notes on how you would deal with this situation.

SAMPLE RESPONSES AND ACTIONS TO EXERCISE 3

"Hello Sir, thank you for coming to see me today. My name is Richard and I am the customer services officer at the centre. I understand there is an issue with a gang of youths outside your shop?" (Establish the facts of the incident by asking relevant questions).

"Can I first of all say that I fully understand how frustrating this must be for you as you are losing customers all the time the problem is present. I wish to apologise unreservedly for any problems that you are experiencing at the centre. I have called the police and they are on their way. In the meantime it is important that I take into consideration your feelings and opinions. Therefore, please can you provide me with some information about what has been happening?" (Make a list of what has happened.)

"How many people are there outside your shop? Has this happened before or is this the first time?"

"Have you reported it to anyone else? Can you provide me with a description of the people who are creating the problem? What type of language are they using?"

"May I reassure you Sir that in line with the code of conduct at the centre will not tolerate any form of anti-social behaviour and we have the power to remove people from the building and prevent them from re-entering at a later point. Whilst we await the arrival of the police I will try to see if the CCTV cameras have picked up anything."

"I am sorry that you have had to go through this experience Sir but we will do everything we can to rectify the problem. As the customer services officer for the centre it is my responsibility to ensure you receive the highest standard of customer care.

With that in mind I will be taking full responsibility for resolving this issue and I will keep you updated of all progress as and when it occurs. Is there anything else I can help you with?"

Notes for sample role-play exercise 3

CHAPTER FIVE

HOW TO PASS THE POLICE SPECIAL CONSTABLE INTERVIEW

Passing the interview is relatively easy. Here's how to pass it:

STEP 1 – LEARN THE CORE COMPETENCIES RELEVANT TO THE ROLE

If you fail to learn the core competencies that are relevant to the role of a police special then you will more than likely fail. Your first step is to obtain a copy of these important attributes. Once you have a copy, you must read them, learn them and be able to provide evidence of where you match each and every one of them.

Anybody can go to an interview and tell the panel that would be a good Police Special, but actually backing this claim

how2become

up with evidence is the key to success. The interview panel want to know that you have experience already in key areas, because if you already have experience in these areas, then you are far more likely to perform well in the role.

The core competencies for becoming a Police Special Constable do change from time-to-time. However, at the time of writing, the following core competencies apply:

- Problem Solving

- Respect for Race and Diversity

- Resilience

- Effective Communication

- Team Working

- Customer and Community Focus

- Personal Responsibility

If the core competencies that you are going to be assessed against during your particular interview vary, do not worry; the process that we have provided you within this section will help you to pass the interview and provide sufficient evidence to match the core competencies.

STEP 2 – PROVIDE EVIDENCE OF WHERE YOU MEET EVERY ASSESSABLE CORE COMPETENCY.

This step is very important, therefore, do not ignore it. When responding to the interview questions that form part of the assessment centre interview, you must provide lots of evidence of where you have already demonstrated the competency being assessed. Let's take a look at a sample Police Special Constable interview question:

Sample question

Provide me with an example of where you have been resilient during a difficult and testing situation?

The above question relates to the core competency of confidence and resilience. Now take a look at a sample response:

Sample response

"Whilst working as a barman in a previous role I was confronted with a difficult and potentially hostile situation to deal with. It was a Sunday afternoon and a large group of men entered the bar after a local football match had ended. They were a group of traveling fans and their team had just been beaten by the home side. Naturally they were disappointed about the result and they wanted to have a drink before catching their train home. Everything was fine for the first half-hour. However, after a while a number of them started to become verbally abusive to a small number of home fans who were drinking in another part of the pub. I started off by asking then men to refrain from using such language. I did this in a calm manner and explained that there were families within the pub too and that this kind of behaviour was not welcome. Despite my pleas they continued to use unwelcome language.

I remained calm and approached the men in a non-confrontational manner. I used open body language and spoke in a calm but firm manner. I informed them that I would not serve them anymore drinks and that they must leave immediately. One of the group began to shout at me stating his annoyance at my stance. I warned him that if they did not leave immediately I would call the police. The men then left the pub and there was no more trouble. I believe it was important to maintain a resilient stance during the situation and to also portray a confident manner. However, I also ensured that I did

not come across in an aggressive or confrontational manner as I believe this would have only made the situation worse."

The above response is an excellent answer to the question for the following reasons:

1. It provides actual evidence of a where a person has demonstrated the core competency of confidence and resilience.

2. The response is detailed in a logical manner, with a beginning a middle and an end. This is important as you will be assessed against effective communication during the interview.

3. The person remains calm throughout the entire scenario and manages to deal with it in a positive manner with a positive end result.

STEP 3 – USE THE S.T.A.R METHOD WHEN RESPONDING TO THE INTERVIEW QUESTIONS AT ASSESSMENT CENTRE.

The STAR method is one that works most effectively when preparing responses to situational type interview questions. We would certainly recommend that you use it during the police special constable assessment centre interview.

The STAR method basically ensures that your responses to the interview questions follow a concise logical sequence and also that you cover every possible area. Here's a breakdown of what it actually means:

Situation

At the commencement of my response explain what the situation was and who else was involved. This will be a relatively comprehensive explanation so that the interviewer fully understands what it is you are trying to explain.

Task

Explain what the task was. This will basically be an explanation of what had to be done and by whom.

Action

Now explain what action you specifically took, and also what action other people took.

Result

Finally explain what the result was following your actions. It is important to make sure that the result was positive as a result of your actions.

Have a go at using the STAR method when creating responses to the sample interview questions that we provide you within this section. Write down the question at the top of a sheet of paper and write down each individual element underneath it.

STEP 4 – WORK ON YOUR INTERVIEW TECHNIQUE

During your pre-interview preparation, concentrate on developing your interview technique. This will involve concentrating on the following key areas:

- Creating a positive first impression when you walk into the interview room.

- Presentation – how you come across to the interview panel.

- Effective communication – how you speak and how you construct your responses to the questions.

- Body language and posture.

- Final questions that you ask at the end of the interview.

- Creating a positive final impression.

The interview will last for approximately 20–30 minutes depending on the length of your responses. During this time you will be asked a number of questions about specific situations and experiences that are important to the role of the Police Special Constable. In relation to the core competency element of the interview there will normally be four questions and you will have just five minutes to answer each of them. Be prepared for additional questions that focus on your reasons and motivations for becoming a Police Special Constable.

These questions will be based around the core competencies and you will be provided with details of these in your information pack, which the police will send you prior to your assessment. The core competencies that are usually assessed at interview are as follows:

- Respect for race and diversity;

- Team working;

- Problem solving;

- Resilience;

- Personal responsibility;

- Customer and community focus;

- Effective communication (not assessed through direct questioning).

In order to ensure you are fully prepared for every eventuality, we will provide you with a sample response to cover every core competency within this section of the guide, with the exception of effective communication. Effective communication is assessed indirectly during the interview. You will be allowed up to 5 minutes to answer each question so don't be afraid to use the time you have.

PREPARING FOR THE INTERVIEW

When preparing for the assessment centre competency based interview you should try to formulate responses to questions that surround the assessable core competencies. The responses that you provide should be specific examples of where you have been in that particular scenario.

SAMPLE INTERVIEW QUESTION BASED AROUND THE CORE COMPETENCY OF PERSONAL RESPONSIBILITY

Question
Please provide an example of where you have taken personal responsibility to arrange or organise an event or situation?

"After reading an appeal in my local paper from a local charity I decided to try to raise money for this worthwhile cause by organising a charity car wash day at the local school during the summer holidays. I decided that the event would take place in a month's time, which would give me enough time to organise such an event.

I set about organising the event and soon realised that I had made a mistake in trying to arrange everything on my own, so I arranged for two of my work colleagues to assist me. Once they had agreed to help I asked one of them to organise the booking of the school and arrange local sponsorship in the form of buckets, sponges and car wash soap to use on the day, so that we did not have to use our own personal money to buy them. I asked the second person to arrange advertising in the local newspaper and radio stations so that we could let the local community know about our charity car wash event, which would in turn hopefully bring in more money on the day for the charity.

Following a successful advertising campaign, I was inundated with calls from local newspapers about our event and it was becoming hard work having to keep talking to them and explaining what the event was all about. But I knew that this information was important if we were to raise our target of £500.

Everything was going well right up to the morning of the event, when I realised we had not got the key to open the school gates. It was the summer holidays so the caretaker was not there to open the gates for us.

Not wanting to let everyone down, I jumped in my car and made my way down to the caretaker's house and managed to wake him up and get the key just in time before the car wash event was due to start. In the end the day was a great success and we all managed to raise £600 for the local charity."

Now that we have taken a look at a sample response, let's explore how the response matched the core competency.

HOW THE RESPONSE MATCHES THE CORE COMPETENCY BEING ASSESSED

In order to demonstrate how effective the above response is we have broken it down into sections and provided the core competency area that it matches.

Sentence

"…I decided to try to raise money for this worthwhile cause by organising a charity car wash day…"

Core competency matched

- Takes on tasks without being asked.

- Uses initiative.

Sentence

"…which would give me enough time to organise such an event."

Core competency matched

- Is conscientious in completing work on time.

Sentence

"I set about organising the event and soon realised that I had made a mistake in trying to arrange everything on my own, so I arranged for 2 of my work colleagues to assist me."

Core competency matched

- Takes responsibility for problems and tasks.
- Takes personal responsibility for own actions.
- Uses initiative.
- Is open, honest and genuine.

Sentence

"…arrange local sponsorship in the form of buckets, sponges and car wash soap to use on the day, so that we did not have to use our own personal money to buy them."

Core competency matched

- Uses initiative.

Sentence

"Following a successful advertising campaign, I was inundated with calls from local newspapers about our event and it was becoming hard work having to keep talking to them and explaining what the event was all about. But I knew that this information was important if we were to raise our target of £500."

Core competency matched

- Focuses on a task even if it is routine.

- Uses initiative.

Sentence

"Not wanting to let everyone down, I jumped in my car and made my way down to the caretaker's house and managed to wake him up and get the key just in time before the car wash event was due to start."

Core competency matched

- Follows things through to a satisfactory conclusion.

- Uses initiative.

- Takes personal responsibility for own actions.

- Keeps promises and does not let colleagues down.

- Takes responsibility for problems and tasks.

The explanations above have hopefully highlighted the importance of matching the core competencies that are being assessed.

When you receive your 'Welcome Pack', make sure you read it thoroughly and prepare yourself fully for the interview. Preparation is everything and by reading exactly what is required you will increase your chances of success on the day.

SAMPLE COMPETENCY BASED INTERVIEW QUESTION 2

Q. Please provide an example of where you have worked as part of a team to achieve a difficult task.

Tips for constructing your response

- Try to think of a situation where you volunteered to work with a team in order to achieve a difficult task. It is better to say that you volunteered as opposed to being asked to get involved by another person.

- Those candidates who can provide an example where they achieved the task despite the constraints of time will generally score better.

- Consider structuring your response in the following manner:

Step 1
Explain what the situation was and how you became involved.

Step 2
Now explain who else was involved and what the task was.

Step 3
Explain why the task was difficult and whether there were any time constraints.

Step 4
Explain how it was decided who would carry out what task.

Step 5
Now explain what had to be done and how you overcame any obstacles or hurdles.

Step 6
Explain what the result/outcome was. Try to make the result positive as a result of your actions.

SAMPLE RESPONSE TO COMPETENCY BASED INTERVIEW QUESTION 2

Q. Please provide an example of where you have worked as part of a team to achieve a difficult task.

"I like to keep fit and healthy and as part of this aim I play hockey for a local Sunday team. We had worked very hard to get to the cup final and we were faced with playing a very good opposition team who had recently won the league title. After only ten minutes of play, one of our players was sent off and we conceded a penalty as a result. Being one goal down and 80 minutes left to play we were faced with a mountain to climb. However, we all remembered our training and worked very hard in order to prevent any more goals being scored. Due to playing with fewer players I had to switch positions and play as a defender, something that I am not used to. However, I understood that the team always comes first and I knuckled down, remembered my training and performed to the best of my ability in the unfamiliar position. The team worked brilliantly to hold off any further opposing goals and after 60 minutes we managed to get an equaliser. The game went to penalties in the end and we managed to win the cup. I believe I am an excellent team player and can always be relied upon to work as an effective team member at all times. I understand that being an effective team member is very important if the police force is to provide a high level of service to the community."

SAMPLE COMPETENCY BASED INTERVIEW QUESTION 3

Q. Provide an example of where you have challenged someone's behaviour that was either discriminatory or inappropriate. What did you do and what did you say?

Tips for constructing your response

- The competency of Respect for Race and Diversity is very important. It is vital you take the time to provide solid evidence of where you meet this area.

- Read carefully the core competency that relates to respect for race and diversity before constructing your response.

- When challenging this type of behaviour, make sure you remain calm at all times and never become aggressive or confrontational.

- Consider structuring your response in the following manner:

Step 1
Explain what the situation was and how you became involved.

Step 2
Now explain who else was involved and why you felt that the behaviour was inappropriate or discriminatory. What was it that was being said or done?

Step 3
Now explain what you said or did and why.

Step 4
Explain how the other person/people reacted when you challenged the behaviour.

Step 5

Now explain what the end result was. Try to make the result positive following your actions.

Step 6

Finally explain why you think it was that the people/person behaved as they did.

SAMPLE RESPONSE COMPETENCY BASED INTERVIEW QUESTION 3

Q. Provide an example of where you have challenged someone's behaviour that was either discriminatory or inappropriate. What did you do and what did you say?

"I recently worked part-time in a local supermarket. One of my colleagues, a lad called Jamie, had special needs. Jamie was an excellent worker who always gave his all during the working day. He sometimes struggled to remember where certain items of groceries were located in the store, but other than this minor issue his work was outstanding.

One day I overheard a customer being rude to Jamie after he struggled to find an item of food the customer has requested. The customers unfortunate gestures had made him nervous and he started to panic. I immediately made my way over to the situation in order to support Jamie and to try and resolve the situation in a calm manner. I started off by standing next to Jamie and telling him that everything was going to be alright and that I would take over from here. I asked the lady what the problem was. She began to explain in an agitated and slightly aggressive manner that Jamie was 'useless at his job' and that he was an 'idiot' for failing to locate the tomato ketchup for here when she requested his assistance.

I immediately challenged her comments and informed her that these comments would not be tolerated. I asked her to take into consideration the fact that Jamie, whilst an exceptional employee, had special needs. I requested that she refrained from raising her voice and to also take into consideration how her actions had made him feel. I made sure that I was polite, tolerant and patient when dealing with the situation but I also ensured that I took into consideration her offending action and how it was making Jamie feel.

She immediately apologised to Jamie for her lack of understanding and inappropriate words. I then told Jamie where he could find the tomato ketchup and he then took the lady along to find the item for her.

Overall I believe this situation was dealt with in an appropriate and successful manner. I managed to prevent the situation from deteriorating whilst maintaining high levels of customer service."

SAMPLE COMPETENCY BASED INTERVIEW QUESTION 4

Q. Provide an example of where you have helped somebody from a different culture or background to your own. What did you do and what did you say?

Tips for constructing your response

- Read carefully the core competency that relates to respect for race and diversity before constructing your response.

- Try to think of a situation where you have gone out of your way to help somebody.

- Try to use keywords and phrases from the core competency in your response.

- Consider structuring your response in the following manner:

Step 1
Explain what the situation was and how you became involved. It is better to say that you volunteered to be involved rather than to say that you were asked to.

Step 2
Now explain who else was involved and why they needed your help or assistance?

Step 3
Now explain what you said or did and why. Also explain any factors you took into consideration when helping them.

Step 4
Explain how the other person/people reacted to your help or assistance. Did they benefit from it?

Step 5
Now explain what the end result was. Try to make the result positive following your actions.

SAMPLE RESPONSE TO COMPETENCY BASED INTERVIEW QUESTION 4

Q. Provide an example of where you have helped somebody from a different culture or background to your own. What did you do and what did you say?

"I was working at a restaurant and noticed a divide between the waiters and kitchen staff. Most of the kitchen staff were older than their waiter colleagues and had migrated from India. There was very little interaction between the kitchen and waiter staff colleagues and I was concerned that this barrier would not only make the kitchen staff feel isolated, but that it would also have a negative impact on the team environment.

My initial considerations were to ensure that the kitchen staff felt comfortable and that they could also speak to me and the waiters if they needed help or assistance. After all, they had not been in the country for long and I wanted them to feel welcome and valued. I believe that communication between colleagues within a workplace is essential to achieve the best possible results and create a good working environment, regardless of individual differences.

To overcome the challenges I introduced myself to all the kitchen staff members and I learnt their names. This ensured that they felt valued and that they also had a point of contact if they ever needed assistance or support. I also encouraged the other waiters to communicate with their kitchen colleagues. Following my actions communication improved and the workplace is now a more efficient and happier working environment."

SAMPLE COMPETENCY BASED INTERVIEW QUESTION 5

Q. Provide an example of where you have solved a difficult problem. What did you do?

Tips for constructing your response

- Read carefully the core competency that relates to problem solving.

- Try to include keywords and phrases from the core competency in your response to this question.

- Consider structuring your response in the following manner:

Step 1
Explain what the situation was and why the problem was difficult.

Step 2
Now explain what action you took in order to solve the difficult problem?

Step 3
Now explain why you took that particular action, and also the thought process behind your actions.

Step 4
Explain the barriers or difficulties that you had to overcome?

Step 5
Now explain what the end result was. Try to make the result positive following your actions.

SAMPLE RESPONSE TO COMPETENCY BASED INTERVIEW QUESTION 5

Q. Provide an example of where you have solved a difficult problem. What did you do?

"I was working in a retail shop and it was a busy trading day in the run up to Christmas. We had been advertising a promotion for a new brand of perfume in the local press that was due to launch the very next day. All of a sudden a member of staff approached me and informed me that no stock of the new perfume had been delivered and that time had run out to get any delivered before the following days trade commenced. This obviously spelt disaster for the company as many people had placed pre-orders of the new perfume and they would be coming in store to collect their goods.

I started off by calling a meeting of three key members of staff. We gathered in the staff room and I co-ordinated a brain storming session in order to resolve the issue. I started off by gathering as much information as possible. The key facts I gained were:

1. *The time we had left in order to get some stock delivered.*

2. *How much stock we needed to fulfil pre-orders.*

3. *Who was available to work late that evening?*

4. *Who had transport and a full driving licence?*

Once I had gathered the facts I then developed a plan to resolve the problem. I asked a member of the team to phone around all company stores in the county to establish which shops had extra stock. I then assigned another member of staff who was willing to work late to drive out to the stores in order to borrow the extra surplus stock. I then personally

placed an initial order with the distributer so that we had enough stock to fulfil orders for the entire Christmas period and to also pay back the stock we had borrowed from other stores in the County.

The result of the situation was that we managed to obtain sufficient stock to fulfil the orders the next day. Finally, I carried out a full investigation as to why this situation had occurred in the first place with a view to making sure it never happened again."

SAMPLE COMPETENCY BASED INTERVIEW QUESTION 6

Q. Provide an example of where you have completed a task despite pressure from others. What did you do and what did you say?

Tips for constructing your response

- Read carefully the core competency that relates to problem solving.

- Try to include keywords and phrases from the core competency in your response to this question.

- Consider structuring your response in the following manner:

Step 1
Explain what the situation was and why you were under pressure.

Step 2
Now explain what steps you took in order to complete the task on time.

Step 3
Now explain why you took that particular action, and also the thought process behind your actions.

Step 4
Explain the barriers or difficulties that you had to overcome in order to finish the task on time?

Step 5
Now explain what the end result was. Try to make the result positive following your actions.

SAMPLE RESPONSE TO COMPETENCY BASED INTERVIEW QUESTION 6

Q. Provide an example of where you have completed a task despite pressure from others. What did you do and what did you say?

"In my current job as car mechanic for a well-known company I was presented with a difficult and pressurised situation. A member of the team had made a mistake and had fitted a number of wrong components to a car. The car in question was due to be picked up at 2pm and the customer had stated how important it was that his car was ready on time because he had an important meeting to attend.

We only had two hours in which to resolve the issue and I volunteered to be the one who would carry out the work on the car. The problem was that we had three other customers in the workshop waiting for their cars too, so I was the only person who could be spared at that particular time. In order to solve the problem I first of all gathered appropriate information. This included exactly what needed to be done and in what priority. I also established what realistically could be done and what couldn't be done in the time-frame given.

I worked solidly for the next two hours making sure that I meticulously carried out each task in line with our operating procedures. Even though I didn't finish the car until 2.10pm, I managed to achieve all of the tasks under pressurised conditions whilst keeping strictly to procedures and regulations."

SAMPLE COMPETENCY BASED INTERVIEW QUESTION 7

Q. Please provide an example of where you have had to make a difficult decision despite pressure from other people.

Tips for constructing your response

- Read carefully the core competency that relates to resilience.

- Try to include keywords and phrases from the core competency in your response to this question.

- Consider structuring your response in the following manner:

Step 1
Explain what the situation was and who was involved.

Step 2
Now explain why the decision was difficult and what pressure you were under.

Step 3
Now explain what you did and why you did it.

Step 4
Explain what the other people did or said in reaction to your decision and explain why you think they reacted as they did.

Step 5
Finally explain what the end result was. Try to provide a positive outcome to the situation.

SAMPLE RESPONSE TO COMPETENCY BASED INTERVIEW QUESTION 7

Q. Please provide an example of where you have had to make a difficult decision despite pressure from other people.

"My son is in his final year at the local school. To date, his work has been exceptional and every parents evening we attend he is praised by his teachers. However, recently there was an incident that involved very poor judgement on my son's part. He got involved with a group of youths from school who were bullying a boy who was less fortunate than themselves. The matter was brought to my attention by the boy's Father. He contacted me by letter and explained that my son had allegedly been involved in the bullying behaviour with the other youths. I immediately asked my son if the allegations were true. He immediately owned up to his part in the bullying, much to the horror of my wife and I.

I decided that the best course of action was to take my son into school and to make the Head teacher aware of the situation with a view for my son to be punished in line with the schools discipline procedures. My wife totally disagreed with my planned course of action and started to put pressure on me to deal with this within the family environment.

However, I maintained my stance. I was determined that my son should be punished by the school first and foremost. By taking this course of action I believed that my son would learn from his mistake and that he would never carry out this dreadful act again. I also wanted to ensure that the other offending youths were punished by the school too, as this would act as a deterrent to anyone else in the school who was thinking of bullying an individual.

Whilst my wife still disagreed with me to this day I believe the course of action I took was appropriate given the seriousness of the situation. My son was punished by the school and has since maintained a very high level of discipline both at school and at home."

HOW TO IMPROVE YOUR SCORES THROUGH EFFECTIVE COMMUNICATION

We mentioned earlier on in the guide that you will be assessed indirectly by effective communication. We will now provide you with some important tips to help you score high in this competency.

During interview, the panel will be looking to see how you communicate and also how you structure your responses to the interview questions.

Consider the following points both during the interview and whilst responding to the interview questions:

- When you walk into the interview room stand up straight and introduce yourself. Be polite and courteous at all times and try to come across in a pleasant manner. The panel will be assessing you as soon as you walk through the door so make sure you make a positive first impression.

- Do not sit down in the interview chair until you are invited to do so. This is good manners.

- When you sit down in the interview chair, sit up straight and do not fidget or slouch. It is acceptable to use hand gestures when explaining your responses to the questions but don't overdo it, as they can become a distraction.

- Structure your responses to the questions in a logical manner – this is very important. When responding to an interview question, start at the beginning and work your way through in a concise manner, and at a pace that is easy for the panel to listen to.

- Speak clearly and in a tone that is easy for the panel to hear. Be confident in your responses.

- When talking to the panel use eye contact but be careful not to look at them in an intimidating manner.

- Consider wearing some form of formal outfit to the interview such as a suit. Whilst you will not be assessed on the type of outfit you wear to the interview, it will make you come across in a more professional manner.

FINAL GOLDEN INTERVIEW TIPS

- Always provide 'specific' examples to the questions being asked.

- During your responses try to outline your contributions and also provide evidence of the competency area that is being assessed.

- Speak clearly, use correct English and structure their responses in a logical and concise manner.

CHAPTER SIX

THE POLICE SPECIAL CONSTABLE FITNESS TEST

The national fitness test has now been introduced in just about every force that requires fitness tests for Specials. More and more forces are introducing fitness tests for Specials and in many cases they are the same as for the regulars. It means it's tougher to get in, but Specials these days perform front-line policing duties most of the time, so this makes sense.

The three elements of this test are:

ENDURANCE (AKA BLEEP/BEEP/SHUTTLE TEST) TO LEVEL 5.4 (DIFFERENT IN SCOTLAND)

During this element you have to run to and fro along a 15 metre track in time to a series of bleeps which progressively

become faster. You have to run as long as possible before you can no longer keep up with the bleeps. You must reach at least level 5.4 in order to pass the fitness test. The total running time is about 3 minutes, 40 seconds. Scotland has a different requirement for their Specials.

DYNAMIC STRENGTH – PUSH 34KG, PULL 35KG

This part of the test is measured on a machine which looks like a large rowing machine with a seat at each end. In the first part of the test, you are pushing against the machine, in the second part, you are pulling against it. You do 3 'warm ups' then 5 maximum force pushes/pulls. You must reach at least 34 kg push strength, and 35 kg pull strength. Grip Strength of 32kg

GRIP STRENGTH OF 32KG

This final part of the test measures the grip strength in your hand using a device called a dynamometer. You grip it in your preferred hand get two attempts to record the maximum grip you can. The pass mark is 32 kg.

Performance on each of these provides a good indicator of your capability of performing various police tasks. The test elements are run consecutively and minimum standards need to be achieved on each.

If you fail to reach the minimum standard in one component of the test, you fail the whole test. If you don't pass the test at your first attempt you can re-take it. However, if you fail the test after three attempts your application will be halted and you will have to wait for at least six months before re-applying.

Although the test is not particularly hard, it does require a certain level of fitness and if you are unfit, out of condition, or overweight, then you may fail this test. Start your preparation as soon as possible and get yourself a copy of the bleep test from www.bleep-test.co.uk.

BONUS SECTION

HOW TO GET POLICE SPECIAL CONSTABLE FIT

INTRODUCTION

Welcome to your FREE 'How to get Police Special Constable Fit' information guide. Within this guide we have provided you with a number of useful exercises that will allow you to prepare for, and pass, the fitness tests.

The fitness test is not too difficult to pass, providing you put in the time and effort to reach a good all round level of fitness. Police Special Constables need to have a good all round aerobic fitness and also a good level of strength and stamina. The exercises contained within this guide will help you to achieve exactly that. Do not spend hours in the gym lifting heavy weights as the job does not require that level

of strength, but rather aim for a varied and diverse fitness programme that cover exercises such as swimming, rowing, jogging, brisk walking and light weight work.

In addition to getting fit, keep an eye on your diet and try to eat healthy foods whilst drinking plenty of water. It will all go a long way to helping you improve your general well-being and concentration levels whilst you prepare for the selection process.

PLANNING YOUR WORKOUTS AND PREPARING FOR THE POLICE SPECIAL CONSTABLE FITNESS TESTS

Most people who embark on a fitness regime in January have given it up by February. The reason why most people give up their fitness regime so soon is mainly due to a lack of proper preparation. You will recall that throughout the duration of this guide the word preparation has been integral, and the same word applies when preparing for the fitness tests. Preparation is key to your success and it is essential that you plan your workouts effectively.

To begin with, try to think about the role of a Police Special Constable and what it entails. You will have to run pretty fast on some occasions and you will also need a level of strength for certain operational tasks. In the build up to the physical tests I advise that you concentrate on specific exercises that will allow you to pass the tests with ease. Read on for some great ways to pass the fitness tests and stay fit all year round.

GET AN ASSESSMENT BEFORE YOU START TRAINING

The first step is to get a fitness test at the gym, weigh yourself and run your fastest mile. Once you have done all three of

these you should write down your results and keep them hidden away somewhere safe. After a month of following your new fitness regime, do all three tests again and check your results against the previous months. This is a great way to monitor your performance and progress and it will also keep you motivated and focused on your goals.

KEEP A CHECK ON WHAT YOU EAT AND DRINK

Make sure you write down everything you eat and drink for a whole week. You must include tea, water, milk, biscuits and anything and everything that you digest. You will soon begin to realise how much you are eating and you will notice areas in which you can make some changes. For example, if you are taking sugar with your tea then why not try reducing it or giving it up all together. If you do then you will soon notice the difference.

It is important that you start to look for opportunities to improve your fitness and well-being right from the offset. These areas are what I call 'easy wins'.

EXERCISES THAT WILL HELP YOU TO PASS
THE FITNESS TESTS

It is my strong belief that you do not have to attend a gym in order to prepare for the fitness tests. If I was applying to become a Police Special Constable today then I would embark on a fitness programme that included brisk walking, running, rowing, presses, sit ups, squats and lunges. In order to improve my upper body strength I would also go swimming.

Walking is one of the best exercises you can do as part of your preparation for the fitness tests. Whilst it shouldn't be

the only form of exercise you carry out, it will go along way to improving your focus and general well being. Now when I say 'walking' I don't mean a gentle stroll, I mean 'brisk' walking. Try walking at a fast pace for 30 minutes every day for a 7 day period. Then see how you feel at the end of the 7 day period. I guarantee you'll begin to feel a lot healthier and fitter. Brisk walking is also a fantastic way to lose weight if you think you need to. In addition to helping you to lose weight it will also keep your concentration and motivational levels up.

There are some more great exercises contained within this guide and most of them can be carried out without the need to attend a gym.

ONE STEP AT A TIME

Only you will know how fit you are. I advise that you first of all write down the areas that you believe or feel you need to improve on. For example, if you feel that you need to work on your upper body strength then pick out exercises from this guide that will work on that area for you. I also advise that you obtain a copy of the multi stage fitness test and practise it. Make sure you can easily pass the required standard.

The key to making improvements is to do it gradually, and at one step at a time. Try to set yourself small goals. If you think you need to lose two stone in weight then focus on losing a few pounds at a time. For example, during the first month aim to lose 6 pounds only. Once you have achieved this then again aim to lose 6 pounds over the next month, and so on and so forth. The more realistic your goal, the more likely you are to achieve it. One of the biggest problems that people encounter when starting a fitness regime is they become bored quickly. This then leads to a lack of motivation and desire, and soon the fitness programme stops.

Change your exercise routine often. Instead of walking try jogging. Instead of jogging try cycling with the odd day of swimming. Keep your workouts varied and interesting to ensure that you stay focused and motivated.

STRETCHING

How many people stretch before carrying out any form of exercise? Very few people is the correct answer. Not only is it irresponsible but it is also placing yourself at high risk from injury. Before we commence with the exercises we will take a look at a few warm up stretches. Make sure you stretch fully before carrying out any exercises. You want your career to be a long one and that means looking after yourself, including stretching! It is also very important to check with your GP that you are medically fit to carry out any form of physical exercise.

The warm-up calf stretch

To perform this stretch effectively you should first of all start off by facing a wall whilst standing upright. Your right foot should be close to the wall and your right knee bent. Now place your hands flat against the wall and at a height that is level with your shoulders. Stretch your left leg far out behind you without lifting your toes and heel off the floor, and lean towards the wall.

Once you have performed this stretch for 25 seconds switch legs and carry out the same procedure for the left leg. As with all exercises contained within this guide, stop if you feel any pain or discomfort.

Stretching the shoulder muscles

To begin with, stand with your feet slightly apart and with your knees only slightly bent. Now hold your arms right out in front of you and with your palms facing away from you with your fingers pointing skywards. Now place your right palm on the back of your left hand and use it to push the left hand further away from you. If you are performing this exercise correctly then you will feel the muscles in your shoulder stretching. Hold for 10 seconds before switching sides.

Stretching the quad muscles (front of the thigh)

Before you carry out any form of brisk walking or running then it is imperative that you stretch your leg muscles. During the fitness tests, and especially prior to the multi stage fitness test, the instructors should take you through a series of warm up exercises which will include stretching the quad muscles. To begin with, stand with your right hand pressed against the back of a wall or firm surface. Bend your left knee and bring your left heel up to your bottom whilst grasping your foot with your left hand. Your back should be straight and your shoulders,

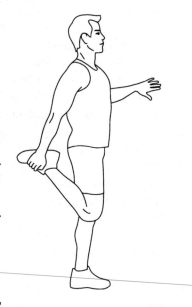

hips and knees should all be in line at all times during the exercise. Hold for 25 seconds before switching legs.

Stretching the hamstring muscles (back of the thigh)

To perform this exercise correctly, stand up straight and place your right foot onto a table or other firm surface so that your leg is almost parallel to the floor. Keep your left leg straight and your foot at a right angle to your leg. Start to slowly move your hands down your right leg towards your ankle until you feel tension on the underside of your thigh. When you feel this tension you know that you are starting to stretch the hamstring muscles. Hold for 25 seconds before switching legs.

We have only covered a small number of stretching exercises within this section; however, it is crucial that you stretch out fully in all areas before carrying out any of the following exercises. Remember to obtain professional advice before carrying out type of exercise.

RUNNING

As I have already mentioned, one of the great ways to prepare for the fitness tests is to embark on a structured running programme. You do not need to run at a fast pace or even run for long distances, in order to gain massively from this type of exercise. Before I provide you with the running programme however, take a read of the following important running tips.

Tips for running

- As with any exercise you should consult a doctor before taking part to make sure that you are medically fit.

- It is certainly worth investing in a pair of comfortable running shoes that serve the purpose for your intended training programme. Your local sports shop will be able to advise you on the types that are best for you. You don't have to spend a fortune to buy a good pair of running shoes.

- It is a good idea to invest in a 'high visibility' jacket or coat so that you can be seen by fast moving traffic if you intend to run on or near the road.

- Make sure you carry out at least 5 whole minutes of stretching exercises not only before but also after your running programme. This can help to prevent injury.

- Whilst you shouldn't run on a full stomach, it is also not good to run on an empty one either. A great food to eat approximately 30 minutes before a run is a banana. This is great for giving you energy.

- Drink plenty of water throughout the day. Try to drink at least 1.5 litres each day in total. This will keep you hydrated and help to prevent muscle cramp.

- Don't overdo it. If you feel any pain or discomfort then stop and seek medical advice.

RUNNING PROGRAMME WEEK 1

DAY 1

- Run a total of 3 miles only at a steady pace.

If you cannot manage 3 miles then try the following:

- Walk at a brisk pace for half a mile or approximately 10 minutes.

Then

- Run for 1 mile or 8 minutes.

Then

- Walk for another half a mile or approximately 10 minutes.

Then

- Run for 1.5 miles or 12 minutes.

Walking at a brisk pace is probably the most effective way to lose weight if you need to. It is possible to burn the same amount of calories if you walk the same distance as if you were running.

When walking at a 'brisk' pace it is recommended that you walk as fast as is comfortably possible without breaking into a run or slow jog.

RUNNING PROGRAMME WEEK 1

DAY 2

- Walk for 2 miles or approximately 20 minutes at a brisk pace.

Then

- Run for 2 miles or 14 minutes.

DAY 3

- Repeat DAY ONE.

DAY 4

- Walk at a brisk pace for 0.5 miles or approximately 7 minutes.

Then

- Run for 3 miles or 20 minutes.

DAY 5
- Repeat day one.

DAY 6 AND DAY 7
- Rest days. No exercise.

RUNNING PROGRAMME WEEK 2

DAY 1
Run for 4 miles or 25 minutes.

DAY 2
- Run a total of 3 miles at a steady pace.

If you cannot manage 3 miles then try the following:

- Walk at a brisk pace for half a mile or approximately 10 minutes.

Then

- Run for 1 mile or 8 minutes.

Then

- Walk for another half a mile or approximately 10 minutes.

Then

- Run for 1.5 miles or 12 minutes.

RUNNING PROGRAMME WEEK 2

DAY 3

- Rest day. No exercise.

DAY 4

- Run for 5 miles or 35–40 minutes.

DAY 5

- Run for 3 miles or 20 minutes.

Then

- Walk at a brisk pace for 2 miles or approximately 20 minutes.

DAY 6

- Run for 5 miles or 35–45 minutes.

DAY 7

- Rest day. No exercise.

Once you have completed the second week running programme, use the 3rd week to perform different types of exercises, such as cycling and swimming. During week 4 you can then commence the 2 week running programme again. You'll be amazed at how easier it is the second time around!

When preparing for the selection process, use your exercise time as a break from your studies. For example, if you have been working on the application form for a couple of hours why not take a break and go running? When you return from your run you can then concentrate on your studies feeling refreshed

Now that I've provided you with a structured running programme to follow, there really are no excuses. So, get out there and start running! I'll now provide you with a number of key targeted exercises that will allow you to prepare effectively for the fitness tests.

EXERCISES THAT WILL IMPROVE YOUR ABILITY TO PASS THE FITNESS TESTS

Press-ups

Whilst running is a great way to improve your overall fitness, you will also need to carry out exercises that improve your upper body strength. These exercises will help you to pass the strength tests which form part of the assessment. The great thing about press-ups is that you don't have to attend a gym to perform them. However, you must ensure that you can do them correctly as injury can occur. You only need to spend just 5 minutes every day on press-ups, possibly after you go running or even before if you prefer. If you are not used to doing press-ups then start slowly and aim to carry out at least 10.

Even if you struggle to do just 10, you will soon find that after a few days practice at these you will be up to 20+.

Step 1

To begin with, lie on a mat or even surface. Your hands should be shoulder width apart & fully extend the arms.

Step 2

Gradually lower your body until the elbows reach 90°. Do not rush the movement as you may cause injury.

Step 3

Once your elbows reach 90° slowly return to the starting position with your arms fully extended.

The press up action should be a continuous movement with no rest. However, it is important that the exercise is as smooth as possible and there should be no jolting or sudden movements. Try to complete as many press ups as possible and always keep a record of how many you do. This will keep your focus and also maintain your motivation levels.

Did you know that the world record for non-stop press-ups is currently 10,507 set in 1980!

WARNING – Ensure you take advice from a competent fitness trainer in relation to the correct execution of press-up exercises and other exercises contained within this guide.

Sit-ups

Sit ups are great for building the core stomach muscles. At the commencement of the exercise lie flat on your back with your knees bent at a 45° angle and with your feet together. Your hands can either be crossed on your chest, by your sides, or cupped behind your ears.

Without moving your lower body, curl your upper torso upwards and in towards your knees, until your shoulder blades are as high off the ground as possible. As you reach the highest point, tighten your abdominals muscles for a brief second. This will allow you to get the most out of the exercise. Now slowly start to lower yourself back to the starting position. You should be aiming to work up to at least 50 effective sit-ups every day. You will be amazed at how quickly this can be achieved and you will begin to notice your stomach muscles developing.

Whilst sit-ups do not form part of fitness tests, they are still a great way of improving your all-round fitness and therefore should not be neglected.

Pull-ups

Pull ups are another great way for building the core upper body muscle groups. The unfortunate thing about this type of exercise is you will probably need to attend a gym in order to carry them out. Having said that, there are a number of different types of 'pull up bars' available to buy on the market that can easily and safely be fitted to a doorway at home. If you choose to purchase one of these items make sure that it conforms to the relevant safety standards first.

Lateral pull-ups are very effective at increasing upper body strength. If you have access to a gymnasium then these can be practised on a 'lateral pull-down' machine. It is advised that you consult your gym member of staff to ask about these exercises.

Pull ups should be performed by grasping firmly a sturdy and solid bar. Before you grasp the bar make sure it is safe. Your hands should be roughly shoulder width apart. Straighten your arms so that your body hangs loose. You will feel your lateral muscles and biceps stretching as you hang in the air. This is the starting position for the lateral pull up exercise.

Next, pull yourself upwards to the point where your chest is almost touching the bar and your chin is actually over the bar. Whilst pulling upwards, focus on keeping your body straight without any arching or swinging as this can result in injury. Once your chin is over the bar, you can lower yourself back down to the initial starting position. Repeat the exercise 10 times.

Squats (these work the legs and bottom)

Squats are a great exercise for working the leg muscles. They are the perfect exercise in your preparation for the fitness tests.

At the commencement of the exercise, stand up straight with your arms at your sides. Concentrate on keeping your feet shoulder-width apart and your head up. Do not look downwards at any point during the exercise.

Now start to very slowly bend your knees while pushing your rear out as though you are about to sit down on a chair. Keep lowering yourself down until your thighs reach pas the 90° point. Make sure your weight is on your heels so that your knees do not extend over your toes. At this point you may wish to tighten your thighs and buttocks to intensify the exercise.

As you come back up to a standing position, push down through your heels which will allow you to maintain your balance. Repeat the exercise 15 to 20 times.

Lunges (these work the thighs and bottom)

You will have noticed throughout this section of the guide that I have been providing you with simple, yet highly effective exercises that can be carried out at home. The lunge exercise is another great addition to the range of exercises that require no attendance at the gym.

To begin with, stand with your back straight and your feet together (you may hold light hand weights if you wish to add some intensity to the exercise).

Next, take a big step forward as illustrated in the diagram making sure you inhale as go and landing with the heel first.

Bend the front knee no more than 90 degrees so as to avoid injury. Keep your back straight and lower the back knee as close to the floor as possible. Your front knee should be lined up over your ankle and your back thigh should be in line with your back.

To complete the exercise, exhale and push down against your front heel, squeezing your buttocks tight as you rise back to a starting position.

Try to repeat the exercise 15 to 20 times before switching sides.

Lateral raises (these work the shoulder muscles)
Whilst Police Special Constables are not usually required to lift heavy items of equipment during their day to day work, they still need to have a good level of upper body strength. Lateral raises will allow you improve your upper body strength in a safe and effective manner.

Take a dumbbell in each hand and hold them by the sides of your body with the palms facing inward.

Stand or sit with your feet shoulder-width apart, knees slightly bent. Do not lean backwards as you could cause injury to your back. Raise your arms up and out to the sides until they are parallel to the ground, then lower them back down carefully. Repeat the exercise 15 to 20 times.

ALTERNATIVES EXERCISES

Swimming

Apart from press-ups, lateral raises and the other exercises I have provided you with, another fantastic way to improve your upper body and overall fitness is to go swimming. If you have access to a swimming pool, and you can swim, then this is a brilliant way to improve your fitness.

If you are not a great swimmer you can start off with short distances and gradually build up your swimming strength and stamina. Breaststroke is sufficient for building good upper body strength providing you put the effort into swimming an effective number of lengths. You may wish to alternate your running programme with the odd day of swimming. If you can swim 10 lengths of a 25-metre pool initially then this is a good base to start from. You will soon find that you can increase this number easily providing that you carry on swimming every week. Try running to your local swimming pool if it is not too far away, swimming 20 lengths of breaststroke, and then running back home.

This is a great way to combine your fitness activity and prevent yourself from becoming bored of your training programme.

Rowing

If there is one exercise that will allow you to work every single muscle group in the body then it is rowing. This is the perfect exercise for preparing to pass the fitness tests. It will increase your aerobic fitness and it will also improve your lower and upper body strength.

As with any exercise of this nature there is a risk of injury. It is crucial that you use the correct technique when rowing on a purpose built machine. By applying the correct technique

you will be far more efficient and you will also see faster results.

Whilst exercising on the rowing machine, make sure you keep your back straight and concentrate on using your legs and buttocks. Never extend so far that you lock out your knees. Try and be smooth throughout the entire exercise. To obtain a suitable indoor rowing training programme that is relevant to your current fitness levels please visit www.concept2.co.uk.

The multi stage fitness test or bleep test
This part of the selection process requires you to demonstrate a specific level of fitness.

In simple terms the bleep test requires you to run backwards and forwards (shuttles) between 2 fixed points a set distance apart. The test is progressive in that as the levels increase so does the difficulty. A tape will be played that contains a series of 'bleeps' set out at different intervals.

The distance between the 'bleeps' at level 1 will be far greater than the 'bleeps' at level 10. Each time the 'bleeps' increase, the tape will let you know that you are progressing to the next level. During the test you will be required to keep up with 'bleeps' and not fall behind them or run ahead of them. Level 1 starts off at around walking pace and gradually increases as each stage progresses.

The best way to practise for this stage of the test is to practise the actual test itself. However, the next best alternative is to go running at least 3 miles, at least 3 times a week. Each time you go out running you should try to push yourself a little bit harder and further.

By running 3 times a week you will give your body the rest it needs in between each run so it is probably best to run on alternate days.

TIPS FOR STAYING WITH YOUR WORKOUT

The hardest part of your training programme will be sticking with it. In this final section of your fitness guide I will provide some useful golden rules that will enable you to maintain your motivational levels in the build up to the tests. In order to stay with your workout for longer, try following these simple rules:

Golden rule number one – Work out often
Aim to train three to five times each and every week.

Each training session should last between 20 minutes to a maximum of an hour. The quality of training is important so don't go for heavy weights but instead go for a lighter weight with a better technique. On days when you are feeling energetic, take advantage of this opportunity and do more!

Within this guide I have deliberately provided you with a number of 'simple to perform' exercises that are targeted at the core muscle groups required to perform the role of a Police Special. In between your study sessions try carrying out these exercises at home or get yourself out on road running or cycling. Use your study 'down time' effectively and wisely.

Golden rule number two – Mix up your exercises
Your exercise programme should include some elements of cardiovascular (aerobics, running, brisk walking and cycling), resistance training (weights or own body exercises such as press-ups and sit ups) and, finally, flexibility (stretching). Make sure that you always warm up and warm down.

If you are a member of a gym then consider taking up a class such as Pilates. This form of exercise class will teach you how to build core training into your exercise principles, and show you how to hit your abdominals in ways that are

not possible with conventional sit-ups. If you are a member of a gym then a fantastic 'all round' exercise that I strongly recommend is rowing. Rowing will hit every major muscle group in your body and it is also perfect for improving your stamina levels and cardiovascular fitness.

Golden rule number three – Eat a healthy and balanced diet

It is vitally important that you eat the right fuel to give you the energy to train to your full potential. Don't fill your body with rubbish and then expect to train well. Think about what you are eating and drinking, including the quantities, and keep a record of what you are digesting. You will become stronger and fitter more quickly if you eat little amounts of nutritious foods at short intervals.

Golden rule number four – Get help

Try working with a personal trainer. They will ensure that you work hard and will help you to achieve your goals. If you cannot afford a personal trainer then try training with someone else. The mere fact that they are there at your side will add an element of competition to your training sessions!

A consultation with a professional nutritionist will also help you improve your eating habits and establish your individual food needs.

Golden rule number five – Fitness is for life

One of my old managers in the Fire Service had a saying – "Fitness Wins!" Two simple words, that meant an awful lot. Improving your fitness and eating healthily are not short-term projects. They are things that should come naturally to you.

Make fitness a permanent part of your life by following these tips, and you'll lead a better and more fulfilling life!

Good luck and work hard to improve your weak areas.